With Wings As Eagles

By
Perry E. Gresham

Anna Publishing Incorporated

The golden eagle on the cover is a copy of a painting by internationally acclaimed writer, artist, teacher and ornithologist George Miksch Sutton. Mr. Sutton was graduated from Bethany College and is a personal friend of the author.

The original watercolor painting is owned by Mr. John E. Kirkpatrick of Oklahoma City. The author is grateful to both artist and owner for permitting the use of this magnificent painting on the cover of this book.

Copyright © 1980
by Perry E. Gresham

Library of Congress Cataloging in
Publication Data

Gresham, Perry Epler.
  With wings as eagles.

  Includes bibliographical references.
  1. Old age—Psychological aspects. 2. Aged—Psychology. 3. Life cycle, Human.
  4. Motivation (Psychology) I. Title.

HQ1061.G72   305.2'6   80-66183
ISBN 0-89305-025-3
ISBN 0-89305-026-1 (pbk.)

Printed and bound in the U.S.A.

Revised   December   1987
Fourth Printing December 1987

CONTENTS

*To our chronologically-gifted colleagues
of Bermuda Village, where we have
discovered enchantment underneath
the Carolina moon.*

*Fierce no more is the spectre of old age
I now see life as a series of renewals
Most are spared senility. It belongs
to disease more than to age
The thrill of renewal can replace depression
Despondency is for those who fail
to find new challenges
Loneliness is for those who fail to cultivate new
friends
Despair is for those who have lost their nerve
I have faced all these spectres
and I have defeated them
With eagle wings I soar above them
Old age is truly better than youth or middle years
I have earned the right to be wise
And to enjoy the inner splendor which has replaced
The external concerns of the busiest years.*

Perry E. Gresham

iv

ACKNOWLEDGEMENTS

Richard Ware, executive director of the Earhart Foundation, was kind enough to read several of these chapters and offer some wise suggestions. The Earhart Foundation, of Ann Arbor, Michigan, provided subvention for research pertinent to the political economy of aging in America.

Paul Poirot, editor of *The Freeman*, was most helpful with many of the ideas. One of the chapters appears under the title, "Liberty for Older Americans," in *The Freeman* for October 1978.

My academic colleagues at Bethany College have been most helpful. John Taylor in English and Pauline Nelson in modern languages read the manuscript and made suggestions for improvement which I have incorporated.

Juanita Mahan, Patricia Napp, Ellen Witham, and especially Karen Atkinson have helped me in the preparation of the manuscript.

My contemporaries, who have brought verve and happiness to their later years, have inspired these chapters. Aleece Gresham, who was the gracious first lady of the campus while I was president, has added still a new dimension of joy and achievement since my retirement.

And although last, but by no means least, I mention Mr. Ike Flores, a long time newsman with the Associated Press. When he interviewed me for a news story on the joys of aging, Mr. Flores read my manuscript. He gave me some very valuable advice out of his interest and out of his years of writing experience. My editor and I were both pleased with his many astute suggestions which we have incorporated into this book.

P.E.G. 1980

INTRODUCTION TO FOURTH EDITION

This is a book for all ages. More than 25,000 people have found their lives brightened and their spirits renewed by having read it. This fourth printing has been revised to reflect new insights and new information which I have found since the original publication.
P.E.G. June 1987

If you are one of the vast majority who are content to fit the stereotype of aging in America
If you wish to some day "grow old gracefully" and get out of the way
If, on retirement, you felt you have earned the right to eat, drink and vegetate
If you do not like to exercise, play and make new friends
If you are too inflexible to get a new image of aging and see life as a series of renewals
Then read no more. This book is not for you. It may even be dangerous to your way of life.

But if you wish to live longer
Have more fun
Do something for humanity
Leave some "footprints on the sands of time"
Then this book is for you!
Read it; begin the best days of your life, and join me as we "mount up with wings as eagles!"

When I started this book I was young old. Now I am old old. I have changed from my early seventies to my late seventies, approaching eighty. I have learned many things. First of all, I have learned that the renewals keep coming and that life can be exciting and wonderful, even when one hits the magic number of fourscore years.

There are some problems of health. I have diseases not different than those of former years, but I have more of them all at once. I think this is characteristic of the old old. I went to my doctor to see about a certain physical problem. He looked me over and concluded that I needed six other doctors! This confluence of many diseases means more time must be spent in coping. It takes longer to see seven doctors than to see one.

In spite of physical difficulties, I have experienced new surges of interest and energy which have enabled me to go on lecturing, writing, teaching and knowing the joy of being alive. I can testify to the truth of the words of Saint Paul when he said, "Though our outward being perish, yet the inward being is renewed day by day" (Second Corinthians 4:16).

My love of life and my joy in living are undiminished. I think that older people can have more fun and can find more delight in life in this period of wisdom and integrity than at any other time throughout one's long existence. My own life is happier, richer and better than at any other time. To be sure, I have many ills. To be sure, I am failing in some respects. My hearing is impaired, my eyes are not good, I do not have quite the versatility in manual dexterity that I once had, but nonetheless I have found that I have gained inwardly what I have lost outwardly. If my eyes are less acute, I know better what to look at. If my hearing is not quite adequate, I know better what to listen to. I have found ways to make up for the loss of sight and sound and to make some very good adjustments to the loss of manual dexterity. If I shake a little bit, it does not keep me from playing golf or dancing. My arthritis tends to create pain occasionally. It does not keep me from covering the four corners of the land giving a message of hope and renewal to my contemporaries. I call to everyone who has reached retirement time and who is going on from young old to old old to join me in the joy and adventure of living by "mounting up with wings as eagles".

One of my students from Africa told me a story which sums up the mood of self-realization which comes to a person who can soar as a golden eagle through the golden years. An old chief found an aerie on a tall mountain. He took the egg of an eagle and brought it down to his own home. There he placed it under a hen. In due time the eagle hatched along with the little chickens. The eaglet thought he was a chicken and the chickens regarded him as a chicken. There was no barnyard warfare between the lone eagle and his siblings.

As time went by the chief thought the eagle should fly, but the eagle enjoyed the security and comfort of the chicken yard. His crooked beak was a handicap for eating grain, but it was very useful on the meat scraps. He continued to grow and develop.

The chief tried to encourage him to fly by pitching him up in the air. The eagle thought it was a game and had great fun soaring back down to feed with the chickens.

One day the chief took his pet eagle up to the top of his tallest building and pitched him into the air. The eagle, now a young adult, simply spread his wings and settled back down to feed with the chickens.

By now the chief was truly exasperated. He took his pet and travelled several miles to the edge of the forest, where he climbed the tallest tree, eagle in hand, and holding on with one hand he threw the eagle into the blue sky of Africa. Those great wings spread out, flapped two or three times and sailed magestically down to the chicken yard! The chief returned to his house puffing and irritated. He picked up his pet eagle, looked him in the eye, shook him and said, "Are you an eagle or are you a chicken? You are a chicken!"—and he threw him down into the chicken pen. The strong young bird was only amused.

That night there came a storm; the kind of violent wind and rain common to the coast of Africa. The chickens were blown up against a building and most of their feathers blown away.

The eagle turned full in the face of the storm and began to fly. He rose up through the clouds out of sight.

The chief expected to see him returning, but he did not come back that night. The next morning the chief thought surely he would return, but when the warm sun came out and the sky was very blue, there was still no eagle. All day the chief was melancholy, for he missed his pet. Something in this young bird evoked a feeling of strength and levitation in the heart of the chief.

Toward evening, a small spot appeared on the horizon. The old chief ran out to watch the spot grow larger and larger as it came from the sunset. Sure enough, it was his eagle!

The chief called to him, stood looking up at him as he sailed once around the chicken yard as if to say goodbye. Then the eagle turned with his powerful eyes fixed on the snow-crowned mountains. He felt the call of liberty and the challenge of the great wide world.

The last time the old chief saw his pet was at that vanishing moment when the setting sun was reflected on those mighty bronze pinions.

With wings as soaring eagles I can fly
I smile to see the rolling clouds go by
Love, life and laughter are my happy way
For this and every other passing day
By blows of circumstance I'm unsubdued
Praise God by love my life has been renewed.

THE SURGE
OF THE SIXTIES

O ne rainy night in St. Louis I hit upon an idea
that changed my entire outlook on life. This
discovery could do wonders for mature people
throughout the world. I awoke from a deep sleep
with a totally new concept of what happens to people who reach that period called "retirement age."

Just before falling asleep that night, I had been
thinking about what I could say to a large assembly of my contemporaries on the subject: "Life
Begins at Seventy." I was not very pleased with
my own ideas and outline. I had prepared a series of
practical suggestions to my friends who, like me,
were confronted with the problems of aging. My
assumptions about the process of growing old were
those commonly held by students of human growth
and development. I had accepted the scenario of
the human life-cycle as childhood, adolescence,
maturity, followed by a plateau which eventually
gives way to slow decline and death.

When I awoke, however, the human pilgrimage appeared to me in a very different and somewhat startling pattern. I felt I had missed the significance of my own experience as well as the implications of the qualities I had observed in my contemporaries.

As I lay there in the dark I saw my own life not as any one peak of achievement, but as three or four peaks with each one appropriate to its particular stage of development. I began to view the progress of a lifetime as three or four surges of energy rather than one rocket burst which reaches its zenith and then slowly falls to its end. I remembered the burst of energy, power and accomplishment which came to me at about the age of thirty. Another high point came at about fifty and kept me going with diminishing velocity on through the middle sixties, when I dealt with the usual problems of retirement from my twenty years as a college president.

Since then I have enjoyed a truly remarkable renewal of power, ability and enjoyment. I have more energy and endurance now than I had at sixty. My judgments are wiser and more reasonable, I believe I dance better, play a better game of golf, accomplish more in my office, give better lectures and find life more exciting than I did when I was in my middle years.

As the sun came up over the Mississippi, I began to ask myself if this was an experience unique to me or if my contemporaries had had similar revelations and experiences. A dozen friends came quickly to mind, tending to confirm my discovery that there is a renewal of power that comes to many in their sixties, and that this comes with enough momentum to carry them on through that last stage of the life cycle. I thought it similar to what athletes call "a second wind."

I have long observed a renewal of sorts in venerable statesmen, business and community leaders, academic colleagues, professional people and an amazing coterie of unsinkable dowagers. My mind, set on conventional concepts of aging, had been blinding me to a new and exciting scenario which could very well turn out to be the greatest discovery of my life. This new idea was like a second sunrise bringing new hope for the later stages. I arose to a whole new world, eager to hurry home, where I could try this theory of a "second wind" on my friends and colleagues. I decided to call this newly identified burst of energy and ability "the surge of the sixties."

I was under the spell of this new discovery as I boarded the aircraft to fly home. The stewardess offered me a magazine as I settled in for the ride. And since I was seated well back in the plane, her supply had dwindled down to the *Reader's Digest.* I was intrigued by the Norman Cousins article, "Anatomy of an Illness." Cousins told the story of his recovery from a particularly difficult illness from which he had cherished little hope of recovery. Now well again, he closed the inspired essay with the paragraph:

> Something else I have learned: never underestimate the capacity of the human mind and body to regenerate—even when the prospects seem most wretched. The life-force may be the least-understood on earth. William James said that human beings tend to live too far within self-imposed limits. It is possible that those limits will recede when we respect more fully the natural drive of the human mind

and body toward perfectibility and regeneration. Protecting and cherishing that natural drive may well represent the finest exercise of human freedom.[1]

This reinforced my concept of a period of renewal in later life. I could hardly wait until I arrived at my office to begin an inquiry into the possibility that I had truly found a whole new approach to the process of growing old.

Back on the campus, I began asking myself the hard question: could it be that I had misread the evidence? Perhaps I had devised a new hypothesis out of nothing more than pleasant association with my friends, a good dinner, a period of rest, and my persistent interest in sending a message of hope to my contemporary friends who are growing older. Perhaps it was nothing more than wishful thinking on my part—a defense against the problems of advancing years conjured up to make me feel better about my own problems. Perhaps it was a temporary feeling of euphoria derived from the fact that I have survived this long in reasonably good health and have enjoyed professional success, laughter, and joy with family and friends. Perhaps it would wear off in a few days and I would be back thinking of life as an ordeal for older people who are trying desperately to hang on to what they have as long as they can, without any hope of ultimate success.

I began my inquiry by reviewing the biographies of the people who have influenced my life and thought, beginning with Plato. I quickly verified the fact that his experiment with politics came after he was sixty. I found also that the great years of his

---

1 Norman Cousins, "Anatomy of an Illness," *Reader's Digest,* June, 1977, pp. 130-134.

Academy, which was really the first university, came in the years of his ripened experience. Six of his greatest Dialogues were written in the two decades before his death at age seventy-nine. His greatest Dialogue, *The Republic,* was written at the age of forty, but it contains at the outset some reflections on old age indicating this great philosopher's expectancy of renewal in later life. He was of the opinion that young people should study no philosophy until they have reached the age of thirty. He saw life as moving from that age into an extended period of wisdom for those who are interested primarily in reason rather than in honor and riches. He said:

> Certainly old age has a great sense of calm and freedom; when the passions relax their hold, then . . . you have escaped from the control not of one master, but of many.

This naturally caused me to inquire about Plato's mentor, Socrates. He died at seventy, condemned by the foolish judges of Athens to drink hemlock as a curious form of execution. The rigged court had accused him of disloyalty to the State and subversion of the young.

Socrates would probably have been lost to history had it not been for Plato and Xenophon, who came to know him in his later years. Both were about forty-five years younger than he. His circle of friends formed a Socratic cult of students and admirers. The old philosopher was past three score when this cult was formed, and Socrates gives evidence of a remarkable surge of energy and power at about that time. He was still in full command of his resources when Athens stupidly put him to death, and because of this made him immortal in history.

Turning to literary people, I thought of Johann

Wolfgang Von Goethe, the great German poet and thinker whose eighty-three years started in 1749. Not only did he experience a renewal in the sixties, but new surges of power kept coming until his death.

Probably the greatest love affair of his life came when he was in his seventies, this time with an eighteen-year-old girl named Ulrike von Levetzow. He courted her with persistence, many gifts and verses. The affair must have brought a new surge of energy, for he was never in better health nor spirits. He wrote some of his greatest poetry shortly after his seventy-fourth birthday, and he danced with all the young girls. His abiding masterpiece, *Faust*, begun at twenty, was finally brought together and published when he was eighty-one. He said in a letter to Eckermann that unusual men "experience a repeated puberty, while other people are young only once."[2]

Some women, even more than men, exemplify seasons of renewal in later life.

Pearl Buck came to be my friend when she was approaching eighty. She gave every evidence of a new surge of insight and power. A commencement address she delivered to our students was memorable for its sparkling and wise pronouncements as well as its stern warnings. She autographed for me the first copy of her new book, *The Living Reed*, fresh from the press. A few years earlier she had written:

> I'm very healthy. And I have an eternal curiosity. Then, I think I'm not dependent on any person. I love people, I love

---

2 Karl Vietor, *Goethe, The Poet* (New York: Russell and Russell, 1970), p. 242.

my family, my children . . . but inside myself is a place where I live all alone and that's where you renew your springs that never dry up.[3]

Each time I see the Red Cross emblem I think of Clara Barton. This remarkable person, who lived to be ninety-one, was sixty when she created the Red Cross. She was all over the world in the service of humanity after that. At eighty-three, she was still going strong but was so annoyed with federal intervention into her voluntary organization that she resigned.

Turning to statesmen, I refreshed my memory of the later years of those two old cronies Thomas Jefferson and John Adams. When Adams was seventy-six and Jefferson was sixty-eight, they began an exchange of letters at a most intimate level. Adams, thinking about Ecclesiastes in the Bible, wrote to Jefferson, "I am not weary of living. Whatever a peevish patriarch might say, I have never yet seen the day in which I could say I have no pleasure; or that I have had more pain than pleasure." When Adams was eighty and Jefferson seventy-two, the older man asked the sage of Monticello, "Would you go back to the cradle and live again your seventy years?" Jefferson responded that he would gladly live again the period from twenty-five to sixty. He would also have like to have re-lived the period after sixty-five when he founded the University of Virginia.

Benjamin Franklin was seventy years old when the Declaration of Independence was signed. That year he went to Paris and did not return until he was seventy-nine. He was active in the Constitutional

---

3 *New York Post.* 1959.

Convention when he was in his eighties. Some of the wisest and saltiest observations belong to the later years of his life when he experienced repeated surges of energy and ability.

Winston Churchill was sixty-six years old when he became prime minister of Great Britain. The Nazi blitzkrieg had engulfed the Low Countries and was bent on conquering all of Europe. The old veteran rose to the challenge of the darkest hour of his country with still more courage and energy than characterized his youth and middle years. In his late sixties, he stood like a colossus astride the British Isles. Around him gathered the military might and the heroic sacrifice that saved the land. The world is better because of this renewal of one amazing personality.

My academic friends and acquaintances have exhibited these same qualities of periodic renewal in later years. John Dewey, for example, brought a new wife to the celebration of his ninetieth birthday. Nicholas Murray Butler, famed President of Columbia University, lived to be eighty-five. Some of his students remember his observation that people who reach a peak of productivity in middle years and then decline continue with that tendency and accomplish little in later life. He contended that those who advance from the middle years seem to grow increasingly productive to the very end. This wise old college president and man of affairs, who guided the university for over forty years through its most remarkable development, wrote in his autobiography, *Across the Busy Years:*

> These reflections indicate, once again, what great advantage Age has over Youth. Age may look back upon years of outstanding happiness and satisfaction which are

accomplished facts. Youth may look forward into an unknown future with hope and confidence, but it will be some time before the history of that future can be known and written.[4]

At this point in my research, I felt compelled to write to some of my contemporaries who are living creative and productive lives after three score years. Back came some exciting answers. A sample of about thirty replies suggests that more than half of them confirm my conclusion that some people experience a renewal of power, health, and ability in their sixties. Several disavowed any experience of periodic resurgence, believing that people who have enough energy keep going a day at a time as long as they live. The remainder found periods of renewal related exclusively to stimulating experiences and challenges. They theorized that a person does what is necessary and that the organism mobilizes to support the effort.

My friends are a diverse lot ranging from dedicated saints to delightful sinners. The blessing of renewal seems to fall alike on both categories. I include here some excerpts from their letters.

Bob Hope responded to my inquiry with wit. Although in his seventies, he writes as if the sixties have just arrived. I share his letter with you:

Dear President Perry:

I enjoyed your letter very much and also your thoughts on the aging process. I think you are absolutely right and there is no doubt about it, a man is in better shape, mentally and physically, in his 60's than he is in his 40's.

I am lucky as I am enjoying great health and due to my activities and my mental exercises, I keep on my toes and find myself walking down the street and breaking into a dance every once in a while.

---

4 Nicholas Murray Butler, *Across the Busy Years*, (New York: Scribner's, 1939), p. 437.

My grandfather lived one week short of 100 years and he also was a very active thinker and exerciser.

I think the more we act like kids the younger we are going to be, at least it is working for me. I'm even thinking of getting a new teething ring . . . for my new set that is! The key is to be happy and feel good and that is up to the individual.

Regards,
BOB

That wise and thoughtful dean of American phychiatrists Dr. Karl Menninger, now in his eighties, responded as follows:

I enjoyed very much your recent letter and the account of your recent insights. You flatter me when you ask me to compare my own experiences. My own 60's were so long ago and so much has happened since, that I can't say anything dependable or wholly accurate about those youthful days. I'm quite prepared, however, to accept your statement quite literally.

Sincerely,
KARL

Colonel Harland Sanders tells of the amazing renewal in his life. He wrote:

"At 65 I was broke and living on Social Security. I was never successful at anything, having been a farmhand, mule tender, locomotive fireman, salesman, ferry boat operator, motel operator and restauranteur.

I was bankrupt at 65 and started franchising a fried chicken recipe I had developed. I peddled it around the country. Many nights I would sleep in my jalopy because I couldn't afford a motel room.

In my 73rd year we showed a profit of $600,000 before taxes. The next year I sold the business for $2 million plus a lifetime salary plus about $100,000 annually from television residuals.

I'm living proof that retirement at any age is nonsense. The Lord said a man should work 'Til thou return to the ground'. That's my intention, and it should be every man's right."

The Colonel, a man of his word, worked until he became fatally ill, dying at the age of 90. May he rest in peace.

Sincerely,
HARLAND

Barry Goldwater, senator from Arizona and my frequent colleague on the platform, beautifully illustrates my theory of renewal in a letter which gives his formula for the golden years.

. . . I have a lifelong philosophy that a person is only as old as he thinks he is or as he wants to be.

I think constant hard work with elimination of any thought of retirement will do more to keep people young than anything I know of. I dread thinking of the time when I will have to retire from politics but, believe me, I am not going to slow down and I think that is why I stay in good shape with my mind as alert as it can be and my enjoyment of the physical things of life is as great as it has ever been.

With best wishes,
BARRY

David A. Werblin exhibited an amazing renewal of power and insight by putting together a great sporting complex in New Jersey. Mr. Werblin, affectionately known as "Sonny" to his intimate friends, retired long ago from the Music Corporation of America. Now he is Chairman of the New Jersey Sports and Exposition Authority.

I do not know whether my comments support your theory or not, but they do honestly represent a candid approach to my activities. Simply stated, I equate motivation with the importance of the challenge. In my own case, I work an average twelve-hour day and have fun doing it, because of the broad scope and variety demanded by my responsibilities as Chairman of the New Jersey and Exposition Authority. I have also found a liking and understanding of young people, and a compulsion, if you will, to pass on a lifetime of practicality, is a great reinforcement of what you call the "surge of the sixties."

Sincerely,
SONNY

Henry Hazlitt, economist, author and columnist, tells about a new attitude which came to him at about sixty. He had written seven books. But his renewed interest in writing something that would endure prompted him to look at the mature years as a time for more worthwhile contributions.

. . . Somerset Maugham has a passage in *The Summing Up* about the compensations of old age: "Paradoxical as it may sound it has more time. When I was younge I was amazed at Plutarch's statement that the elder Cato began at the age of eighty to learn Greek. I am amazed no longer. Old age is ready to undertake tasks that yough shirked because they take too long." In other words, some older men realize that their time is running out and concentrate their efforts on the things they consider most worthwhile. So it has been for me a surge of ambition, a re-direction of energy, rather than a new surge of energy that develops . . .

Sincerely,
HARRY

Lawrence Fertig, widely known columnist with the old *Herald Tribune* in New York and celebrated author of several books in the field of economics writes:

> Your "second wind" theory about the energy of old-timers is really most interesting. I have the feeling that there is some substance in your idea about those in their 60's and 70's—with one proviso. The essential ingredient is for the individual to assume some new responsibility, to engage in some absorbing activity, and to get the hell out of his house and stop worrying about his health, his assets and his safety in this disturbing world.
>
> In other words, if a man as he grows older will only give his inherent energies a good chance to express themselves he will, I think, feel a new "surge of powers," as you so aptly express it. . .

As ever,
LARRY

Testimony to the surge of the sixties comes from all quarters of life.

The Right Reverend Allen J. Miller, Bishop of Easton, Maryland (retired), who was chaplain to both Presidents Roosevelt and Eisenhower, writes:

> Retirement brings both joy and apprehension: relief from the burden of labor and concern regarding the use of one's new found freedom. I faced this emotional paradox at age sixty-seven when I resigned my jurisdiction. I had been an active bishop and had enjoyed the challenge and responsibility of my office. Separated from my diocese and its demands upon my life forced me to seek means of remaining active. First, I assisted bishops of other jurisdictions. This helped. But I soon found that there was a continuing hunger within to exercise in a helpful way whatever talents had been given me. Two things just

seemed to happen at this point: (1) I found myself deeply involved in a renewed study of the Greek New Testament and (2) I helped organize a study group whose interests became identified with the teachings of Jesus as related to a life of prayer. Five years have now gone by. I must testify that I have been given renewed strength and insight to do research, to teach, to counsel and to learn something more about the admonition to 'pray without ceasing.' By way of testimony: I have never been happier nor more deeply committed to what I have learned anew to be my ministry. I find my days full with effort to emulate this new Christian, whom I see as a continuing reminder of God. I no longer think of time, nor of the vulnerability usually attached to aging. I simply keep enjoying my new life of sharing. All this makes me wonder if there are not moments along life's way when we are confronted by what we may call experiences of rebirth!

Dr. Maurice Brooks, Dean of the College of Forestry, West Virginia University (retired), who is an authority on the Appalachians and author of the beautiful book, *The Appalachians:*

I, too, experienced something of what you describe as rejuvenation around seventy. I retired from teaching at sixty-nine, in 1969. Almost immediately I went to work for the West Virginia Antiquities Commission, as Research Analyst for the investigation of possible sites for the National Register of Historic Places. The work was interesting, we visited many places and became acquainted with many people. I felt as though I had embarked on a whole new career.

We have a fairly large and productive garden, and I found that I was working more easily, and with greater efficiency, than for years previously. Ruth and I still do some fairly strenuous hiking. A couple of years ago we hiked up the Pinkham Notch Trail to Tuckerman Ravine, on Mt. Washington. One of the bright young hut boys looked at my gray hair, and remarked, 'How in the hell did you get up here?'

I retired once more in 1974, but I go to my office almost every day we are in Morgantown; I'm still doing a lot of writing, and just now rejoicing in our first grandchild.

13

With Wings As Eagles

The London Times carried the story of Leopold
Stokowski's death at age 95. The story mentioned his
slender and graceful hands, his mane of white hair
and his musical genius that made him one of the
world's greatest conductors.

"For sixty years he was a recording artist and celebrated
that anniversary by conducting the London Philharmonic in
Brahm's Second Symphony.

After his development of the Cincinnati, Philadelphia and
Houston Orchestras, at age 80 he founded the American Symphony Orchestra of New York for the benefit of talented
youth.

The renewal that came at the time most people retire carried him to the very peak of his career. He earned $250,000
a year from guest conducting, radio and television appear-
ances, record royalties and opera performances. He was
already 80 years old when he was divorced from Gloria
Vanderbilt, his third wife. This great musical hero was still
on the podium with spotlights playing on his white hair and
graceful hands when he was in that last notable performance
in London. He was, at that time, about to record
Rachmaninoff's Symphony No. 2 under a six-year contract
with CBS.

James Aker, a traveling evangelist of Lynchburg,
Virginia, was nearly blind at the age of 112 years. Dr.
Kerry Woodruff performed surgery and restored sight
to this remarkable exemplification of renewal in later
years. The good Lord's sky pilot described his recovery
by saying, "I'm not retiring — I'm refiring!"

W. Arthur Rush, Hollywood executive producer and
artist's manager who developed such celebrities as
Nelson Eddy, Roy Rogers and Dale Evans:

I agree with your discovery 100%. Now that you remind
me I am definitely aware that I experienced the thirty, fifty
and seventy changes. I honestly believe that age seventy has
been the most exciting period in my long career.

I hit seventy on April 2, 1977. I took my annual physical
hostly thereafter. My physician is rated among the best in
the medical profession here in the San Fernando Valley. Many
of the top physicians, surgeons and their families are patients
of his. Dr. Anderson told Mary Jo that I was in the best
physical condition (at my age) of all his patients.

14

As you are aware, I have been an executive throughout my long career in the entertainment industry. I was still in my twenties when I was head of RCA Victor and Columbia Management of California for CBS. Art Rush, Inc. is thirty-eight years old and still very active. Through the years I have been the founder and executive director of several other corporations. The responsibilities and so-called frustrations in dealing with temperamental stars were sometimes awesome. By the time I reached thirty, I was married and raising a family. Mary Jo and I celebrated our forty-second wedding anniversary last October 28th. I was so involved in my work I really never thought about the thirty period.

At age seventy I find myself in excellent health and my business seems more active than in previous years. I actually never thought about retiring at age sixty-five. Of course, I own my own business and maintain my own schedule. I even work on Saturday and Sunday mornings quite often. I still produce all the shows for my clients and travel extensively with them.

Frederick Hauck is in his early nineties. He is the pride of Cincinnati, Ohio, and Winter Park, Florida. His versatility appears when one considers that he is an engineer, inventor, musician, entrepreneur and philanthropist.

I came to know this genius through my friend, Darrell Wolfe, who told me of Dr. Hauck's invention of a nuclear-powered engine which is light, efficient and clean. Most of the work on this engine has been completed since Dr. Hauck was 75 years old.

When he received the Wings As Eagles Award from Bethany College, it read as follows:

FREDERICK A. HAUCK

Rara Avis

MIGHTY EAGLE who rises above the earth
to scan the universe
He remembers humanity on this little blue planet

PROMETHEAN GENIUS who brings down fire
from Olympus
In his hands it becomes speed and transportation

MODERN LEONARDO DA VINCI of the liberal arts

philanthropist who loves all mankind

WISE OWL for whom age is irrelevant and life is joy

... I am resurging each 14 hour day—ruddy of cheek, clear of eye, fast on my feet and happy in my heart—my soul filled with faith—a believer in God's assurances and grateful for the wonderful challenging years I've experienced on this good earth.

Leonard Dalsemer, president of the John A. Hartford Foundation (which has given away more than two hundred million dollars in the last ten years), is at the apex of his powers in his seventies and writes:

I find the challenges I have now, which have, of course, been picked out through my own choice, more exciting and stimulating than many of those that were forced on me as part of the repetitive heavy daily responsibilities of major corporate life ... I am more relaxed and probably I am enjoying more than ever before my involvement in business, financial and philanthropic matters.

Cecil H. Green, the genius who put together Texas Instruments and who becomes an octogenarian in 1980, agrees with Barry Goldwater and Bob Hope that both physical and mental activities enhance the length of one's useful life:

Ida and I have always walked together, going back to before we were married in 1926. Thus, decades ago we walked religiously every day and even though in those early days such activity was considered a waste of time by most of our friends ... I am likewise impressed that mental activity is equally necessary, for it seems that the brain cells need stimulating exercise as much as our muscles.

I am thankful that at the outset of my professional career I became involved in a company which has been completely dependent upon innovation in a realm of high technology. So, it became practical and indeed necessary, to engage in the pleasurable pastime of industry-education relationships ... It seems that this wonderful relationship has no age limit and so I find myself as busy as ever in developing new and fresh industry-education working relationships.

After reviewing the literature in the field, taking a fresh look at the biographies of famous people, talking with my contemporaries and reflecting on the problems, I have arrived at this conclusion: Life is a series of renewals rather than a machine that wears out a little at a time. The Sanskrit maxim, "The view depends upon the point of view," is relevant. We have deceived ourselves into thinking of human life in mechanical terms.

Our language betrays this tendency. We speak of growing old and imply the kind of obsolescence that comes to an old automobile. When we wish to compliment someone for health and vigor, we say, "You look young," which presumes that this rare person has been able to hold onto his youth; when the fact is that he has experienced some renewal in his later years. Goethe was right when he saw himself as renewed rather than still young, and when he implied that older is better. Ponce de Leon was doomed to failure when he looked for the Fountain of Youth. Had he searched for the Fountain of Age he could have found it within himself.

The great Harvard physician of the last generation, Dr. Richard Cabot, wrote an essay called "Vis Medicatrix Dei" in which he shows the amazing power of the human organism to renew itself. This great power operates, he said, only for those who know how to provide the conditions. Those who want to enjoy creative renewal in later years must lift the level of their expectancy. People tend to do what is expected of them. Those who expect to do so wear out a little at a time until death claims them.[5]

Those who have learned how to have their strength renewed "mount up with wings as eagles."

---

5 Cabot and Dicks, *Art of Ministering to the Sick.* (New York: Macmillan, 1936), p. 118.

The late Justice Thomas Clark of the Supreme Court sent this handwritten note to me on the day before his death.

> It was kind of you to send me the quote from Norman Cousins. It is something to conjure over; the 'natural drive ... toward perfectibility and regeneration' often results in self-imposed limits on individual livelihood; but, generally, one whose thoughts are worthy places no limits on them. He feels free as the bird.

Periods of creative renewal are related to stimulating situations and challenges. The human being mobilizes to a specific situation in a mysterious and resourceful way. Rudyard Kipling had this in mind when he wrote the little story about the kangaroo that jumped clear over the ocean because "he just had to."

The person who finds the Fountain of Age has learned how to utilize his experience and insight. He knows how to stay well, avoid excesses, arrange his priorities, and relate himself to productive situations. The person who makes the same mistakes over and over again through his life can expect very little bonus of renewal as he enters the fourth period called the age of wisdom and integrity.

Ernest Ligon, who has spent a lifetime studying the attitudes and traits that make for achievement and happiness, has pretty well wrapped it up in three propositions:

THINK TRUTH

LIVE LOVE

TRUST GOD

When I wrote to Dr. Ligon about the surge of the sixties, he replied with an interesting report which is also a testimonial:

Some years ago in the American Psychological Association, Section of Gerontology, research was done which demonstrated that if a person continued to use his mind after graduation from college, he never experienced the retardation that comes to people who have not done so. As you know, I have just passed my eightieth birthday, and I can say with some competence, that there are times when my mind seems to run at full tilt. There are others when it does not. What the future will bring for me, remains to be seen. I come from a long-lived family, and may very well be around until ninety, which so many of my forebears have done. I ought to be able to give you a good deal of more direct evidence, at least as to what has happened to one mind during those ten years.

Three months have passed since that night I spent in St. Louis. My new vision of later life is even brighter now than when the morning sun came up over the Mississippi. I cannot promise anyone a period of renewal such as I have enjoyed. This, however, I have learned for sure: a remarkable surge of power and ability came to me in the sixties and has come, in similar fashion, to many of my closest friends. Some of my colleagues now in their eighties have indicated that these periods of renewal recur from time to time for as long as one lives. I have carefully studied the scientific literature of gerontology, and I have found nothing that refutes my experiences.

The famous Swiss psychiatrist, Carl G. Jung, hinted at a basis for renewal in later life as he considered the different ways in which growth occurs in youth and age. He expressed the sage opinion that perceptive people find within themselves, in the afternoon of life, the qualities of meaning that youth finds in the world outside.

19

I say to you, friend and contemporary, find something meaningful to do, safeguard your health, live with moderation, provide the conditions, and the great scripture will be fulfilled in your life as it is in mine. "But they that wait upon the Lord shall renew their strength; they shall mount up with wings as eagles; they shall run, and not be weary; and they shall walk, and not faint." (Isaiah 40:31)

AGING IN AMERICA

Older Americans are in a serious identity crisis. Many of the current conceptions of aging are not appropriate for bright and active older people. The norms are changing, too, and this adds to the problems of identity. The acceptable role for grandparents, "senior citizens," and "older Americans" is anything but clear; but even when it is clarified, it turns out to be objectionable to any person who has a mind of his own. Most of us do not fit the stereotypes that have accumulated through years of misunderstanding.

Now that I am older, I sense in American life a sort of contempt for the old. I have tried hard to make allowances for any hypersensitivity or personal idiosyncrasies; but the stark fact of contempt still remains. Old people are often regarded as a nuisance. The prevailing attitude seems to be, "Get out of the labor force and leave room for the young," or "Get off the highway and let the young people who wish to go somewhere, go. These things cannot possibly mean anything to you so get out of the way and let us enjoy them."

I have noticed a look of irritation and contempt when I must ask some mumbling young person to repeat a sentence because I do not clearly understand what he is saying. When a young person spills his coffee, it is just a mistake; but when I spill mine, it is because I am shaky and old. The doctors say, "At your age you should not undertake this kind of treatment," or an onlooker will say, "Just look at the old fool trying to be romantic." Once it was said that children should be seen and not heard. This same attitude of contempt has now been transferred to older people. The attitude seems to be, "Shut up, Dad. Things have changed since you had anything to do with them."

This attitude does not always have a hostile edge. It may be a benign compassion—which increases the intensity of the sting. It is easier to face contempt than such an attitude as "Oh, there, there, now; of course you feel that way because you are old." A person who is pitied is diminished in self-respect far more than a person who is scorned. Members of one's own family may be swept up in the conventional attitudes toward aging to the extent that they exhibit a condescending attitude toward anyone past sixty-five.

What could be more infuriating to a highly competent older person than to have one say, "How remarkable! You still drive a car?" or "You are in your seventies. Do you still give lectures?" There are times when those of us who are old need sympathy and pity and we do well to accept it with grace and gratitude; but there are other times when we deserve respect, and we resent being exposed to the so-called "compassion for the old." This is about the most obnoxious attitude anyone could hold toward us. When we are capable and qualified, we should be regarded as equals when appropriate and as superiors where we deserve it. But in every case, we have the right to stand on our own feet and be treated as honorable, respected people.

My students think of me as a friend and teacher rather than as an old man. Their lives are identified with mine. I look upon my students as junior colleagues. I do not think of them as young but as friends who are like me, trying to learn. This is a beautiful relationship. Marcus Aurelius began his meditations with praise of his teachers. Confucius wrote one of his most cherished paragraphs in praise of his students. When everyone was talking about the generation gap, I answered in the words of one of my lighthearted friends, "I have no trouble with the generation gap. I get along fine with old people."

I have found that there is more antipathy between the generations than I had previously thought. My oldest brother, in his middle eighties, has recently remarried. He was temporarily in Colorado Springs. I was lecturing in Denver, and hoped to have a dinner party in honor of the bride and groom. I rented a car to drive down to Colorado Springs to entertain them. As I left the airport, I had to pull into the traffic. I made a left turn. It impeded the flow of traffic somewhat, but not any more than was necessary. Right back of me appeared a pick-up truck with three young people who rolled down the windows, crowded me to the curb and began to shout, "Die, old people! Old people, Die!" I was confused and shocked, and I confess, a bit angry. After two or three blocks they went their way and I drove on toward Colorado Springs. While driving along, I realized that they were probably responding to the printed remark of Governor Lamm of Colorado who had been wrongly-quoted as saying, "It is the duty of old people to die". I wrote to him and told him this story. He apologized for the rude behavior of some of his young citizens, and explained to me that he had simply said that when a person is effectively dead with no awareness and no hope of recovery, it is the duty of that person to die, rather than to be kept alive as a vegetable at public expense.

Nevertheless, it indicated a great deal of hostility on the part of these young people toward us old people. I had not realized before that my sparse gray hair and my weatherbeaten face could bring about a death wish on the part of some young people who thought it was my duty to die and get off the highway. I have found some similar attitudes of hostility on the part of old people toward the young.

Often when an older person goes out to get work, the employment counselor shakes his head and says, "Oh, too bad. You are sixty-six years old." The public assumes that old people are incompetent workers. This is just plain false. Some people are incompetent at any age, and it is only fair to admit that some, even many, old people are incompetent workers. But the principal factor involved is not age. A young ass is no less incompetent that an old one. When older people are capable, they also have the great advantage of experience and work habits that get directly at the issue. It is fascinating to look at the performance record of older scholars, for example.

Wayne Dennis, Professor of Psychology at Brooklyn College, published the results of his interesting study of creative productivity between the ages of twenty and eighty in the *Journal for Gerontology,* 1966. He found that historians produce more notable works in their sixties than in any other decade, with only a modest decline for the seventies. The same tendency toward achievement in later life holds for philosophers and scholars in general. In the field of science, the contributions of major works on the part of those in their sixties and seventies was, though less striking, still very impressive. Inventors, for example, did better by far in their sixties

24

and seventies than in any other decades. In the arts, however, the thirties and forties fared better, although novelists, chamber musicians and poets achieved more in later years.

A little bit of common sense will tell any reflective person that many people have a whole new surge of vitality, interest and ability in the sixties. This is particularly true for people in public life, those in business, the professions and finance. The stereotype of the spent old person at sixty is about one hundred percent wrong. Yet, older people face major discrimination when they attempt to market their talents. I have been shocked by my contemporaries in law and medicine—still active in their professions—who say to me, "Oh, at your age, I do not think you should take on anything else." Here are intelligent people, who would not give up their own responsibilities for anything, advising their patients and clients to live by those old-fashioned concepts.

These norms, however, are changing. Once the old people in America were few, but now we are many. With the increase in life expectancy and the interesting configuration of population growth, old people have come to be a powerful political force. Now, eleven percent of the American people are past sixty-five. As the numbers have increased, so have the skills and methods of political clout. Many old people have come to be active exponents of a minority seeking a voice in public affairs. The large associations of people in their sixties-plus are as numerous and active as any associations in America. A new breeze is blowing through the mulberry trees.

Congressman Claude Pepper, approaching eighty, introduced legislation to lift the mandatory retirement age from sixty-five to seventy. This perceptive

Alabama-born lawyer was old enough to know what mandatory retirement at sixty-five could do to some people and vigorous enough to do something about it. His influence in the House Committee on Aging not only found expression in a law beneficial to many older people, but increased the awareness of his fellow Congressmen concerning the needs of older people. They were astute enough to understand the new political power of the people who are sixty-plus. Senator Pepper would have made a still greater contribution if he could have persuaded his colleagues in Congress to reduce government control of our private lives in order that we could employ and be employed as we please just as long as we do not by force or fraud injure our fellows.

Gordon F. Streib, Professor of Sociology at Cornell, has studied the aged to determine if they have the characteristics of a minority group. He arrived at a negative conclusion for a number of reasons. They are not a distinct class—stereotyped by people in a certain way, denied access to the good things of life—because of special characteristics they hold in common. Aging people are a very heterogeneous lot. Nevertheless, they have enough characteristics and interests in common to make a substantial political difference in the country even though they differ widely from one another in their interests and loyalties in politics, economics and general culture.[1]

Some of the points I make here may be widely disputed, as I find myself disputing some of the most vigorous attempts of some aging activists to get special interest legislation approved by Con-

---

1 Gordon F. Streib, "Are the Aged a Minority Group?" in *Middle Age and Aging*, Bernice L. Neugarten, ed. (Chicago: University of Chicago Press, 1968, p. 35ff.

gress. The privilege of differing viewpoints is certainly an earned prerogative of the mature. When I say we want these things, I really mean that these are the things that seem, to me, paramount for those of us who have reached the sixties.

LIBERTY

Who has earned the right to personal and political freedom more than a person who has lived through six or seven decades?

Some people do not like liberty, and some have become so inured to tyranny that oppression seems comfortable. Taking all this into account, I am still convinced that I speak for my contemporaries when I say we dislike all these so-called "mandatory" programs that affect our lives. We dislike arbitrary retirement, unfair discrimination with regard to our earning power without losing income from the Social Security insurance we have purchased and the unjust discrimination written into the income tax which denies an older professional person deductions for activities that preserve his image and confidence as a professional. We don't like arbitrary laws that bar him from gainful employment or legal restrictions that forbid fair access to the good things of life enjoyed by other people. Nothing could be more distasteful than a law requiring a person to work, or not to work, until a certain age—regardless of what that age might be. What is wanted is freedom to work as long as one wishes and for as long as anybody wishes to employ him.

This same resentment against the loss of individual liberty holds for such things as the consumer movement when it affects senior citizens. No self-respecting old person prefers decisions out of Washington to those of his own taste and inclination. It should be my privilege to choose the food I wish to buy. Nothing infuriates me more than to pay taxes, against my will, to employ some pretentious ass to sit at a desk in Washington and tell me what I should purchase. I find the whole idea revolting, and many of my contemporaries feel the same way.

I keenly resent being told what kind of car I can drive, when I can drive it and how fast, assuming, of course, that I stay within the bounds of propriety of what is right and decent and safe for everybody involved. Even more keenly, I resent being told what drugs I am free to purchase. It is the duty of government to require clear labeling and to vigorously prosecute those who, by force or fraud, misrepresent any product. It is most certainly not the function of the government to forbid me the use of saccharin, for example, when I have been told what is involved in using it. The paternal "Papa knows best" attitude of the Food and Drug Administration is infuriating to all of us who have been around for a while.

I greatly admire Maggie Kuhn and her astonishing success in organizing the Gray Panthers. I could not agree with her more with regard to "those rotten myths" about old people. We are not all alike. We are not all crochety, with shriveling brains and diminishing gender.

However, I have far less faith in government to solve our problems than has she. She appears to be pressing for a consumer movement with a new government bureau for consumer advocacy. This will only produce another layer of bureaucracy and inflation, thereby damaging all of us who are aging. I long for individual liberty; not benign regimentation until I am taxed into penury. I believe many of my contemporaries feel the same way. The only march against the government I would lead would be one which bears a placard, "Get Off Our Backs." We would be perfectly able to solve our own problems if we had some liberty and could get some relief from inflation.

FREEDOM TO WORK

I am well aware of the need for companies, universities and bureaucrats to have a retirement policy. I have great respect for corporations and institutions which prepare people for retirement and offer incentives to make it attractive. I am also aware of the damage that can be done to an individual by any kind of arbitrary, mandatory retirement policy that brings about destructive loss of dignity and self-esteem for an individual. A most poignant illustration is the untimely death of my lifelong friend, Don Gillis, a composer, symphony conductor and network broadcaster of considerable ability and public esteem.

Gillis was arbitrarily retired against his will, and brought suit against the state university where he had been employed. His resentment and sense of injustice were deep and emotional. Although the legal action was far from settled at the time of his death, he had rationalized himself into a promising, alternative course of action a few months before a fatal heart attack. How much the anguish of forced retirement had to do with his death no one can say. One of his last creations was "The Throwaway Generation," which I print by his permission, given before his death:

THE THROWAWAY GENERATION

Somewhere in between the tick and the tock of the twelve o'clock hour that separates midnight from the dawn, I moved from being real to make-believe, from being useful and productive to being out of step with our society.

Instant obsolescence, that's what the moment was!

Being "sixty-five and still alive" meant being shelved, put out to pasture, forced to retire, reduced to being part-time citizen, and I didn't like the thought too much.

But civilization decreed it should be so because retirement based on birthdays is an administrator's dream—no need for conscience here, we've got iron-clad rules!

So with the birthday, all the regulatory forces of the system set themselves in motion to transform virility into emasculation for a human soul who would just as soon keep on keeping on.

What is the thing that happens in that tick and tock that changes you from being sixty-four to sixty-five?

Does the psyche collapse?

Does physical strength vanish?

Does the will to "do" shrivel away?

Do we become invisible in society's eyes?

Do we, for all intents and purposes, perish from the earth?

Cannot a society which has worked such miracles as going to the moon and sending pictures back from Mars solve the problem of what to do with oldsters?

Or should I say the "useless" oldsters, the "obsolescent" oldsters, the "hang-around-doing-nothing" oldsters, the "mandated" ones, the "folks-who-lost-their-constitutional-rights-because-a-birthday-came" oldsters?

True or false?

All men are created free and equal until their sixty-fifth birthday.

Lucky for us we're only obsolescent, not disposable in the way most other products have been made to use and throw away.

Instant obsolescence!

Better say it like it is: instant oblivion!

It isn't such a happy situation when you get the feeling you'd be more respected as a memory than as a living, breathing being.

Yet it happens, and it happens all the time.

We who occupy this earthly space so well until our sixty-fifth birthdays are rewarded with a thing they call retirement and, with a swift and terrible suddenness we find ourselves no longer needed.

We are denied our dignity.

Our right to do is wrenched away by fiat.

Our cup runneth under.

We are members of the generation they've thrown away as being useless and embarrassing. We are the little old ladies and dirty old men, senior citizens whose honors include discounts at drugstores and Disney movies (if accompanied by a child).

We are one-third of a nation and yet they try to hide us away in rest homes and geriatric wards. We hold the wisdom of past centuries in our active minds, yet they let it drain away in uselessness.

They make us into caricatures on TV commercials, portray us nostalgically in symbols of gentle foolishness, as oldsters gumming our geritol-flavored pacifiers.

We are statistics now, where once we were the nation's heartbeat. We upset them now because we're still alive, contrary to the actuarial tables which predicted that we wouldn't be around.

We are of value only if to prove that we are living longer and staying on where once we just lay down and died.

Not any more!

The product which they thought would obsolesce and go away simply won't conform.

Each year while heads grow greyer (although they needn't—courtesy of chemistry) and wrinkles deepen (although cosmetic surgery outdoes Ponce de Leon) more and more of us grow less and less dependent.

That's not quite true.

We grow less dependent on a thing called children. Old daddy gov'mint stepped right in and shooed the kids away.

"We'll take care of your pappy and mammy for you," the politicians said.

And so they did with floods of "care" like Medicare and "ades" like Medicade.

Need medicine?

We'll pay.

Just fill out this form.

Need dentures or a doctor?

Hang in there, fill this out, do it in triplicate.

Need some crutches or a cane?

Turn on tee-vee, Grampa, Washington give it all free.

And as for you, Gramma, I'll be blamed if those biscuits don't taste almost like you made the batch from scratch!

Need a lift?

We'll haul you to the doctor or to the church of your choice regardless of race, creed or national origin.

Want some fun?

We have this place where you can play cards all day or string some beads or make some moccasins. Yes, folks, Community Love, Inc. will haul you to the shopping center to help you spend your food stamps, get your shots, or buy your pills. And every now and then we'll have a dance at Old Age Plaza. Admission free if you're over sixty-five.

On and on it goes.

Need this?

Want that?

Take this!

Sign that!

The broth is spoiled by all the cooks who hold down well-paid jobs to make us think that they're concerned. Care (nowadays) is only the last syllable of a government handout.

They (our government-funded nannies) are caretakers for millions, not caring *for* (really) or even caring *about*—just caretaking ... the kind of caretaking folks do who keep our cemeteries neat.

... pre-fatal care ... as once pre-natal care prepared us for an entry from the womb to begin the journey to our tomb.

We are studied by a friendly government.

And the news is in.

We are one-third of that government, but it matters little to them. They study us with giant grants to universities, to research centers, to church and civic groups.

And they publish, spewing statistics signifying nothing. Statistics never smile nor give a gentle backpat.

We are obsolete, America . . .

And even worse . . .

We are an endangered species!

But they are endangered more!

Look at what you're doing to yourself, America!

Imagine trying to function with one-third of your body gone. Imagine trying to think with one-third of your brain missing.

In an energy crunch, we waste one-third of our national potential because it has been made socially incompatible, it is retired and over-aged.

If you are a senior vice-president, you are a highly respected business leader.

But if you are a senior citizen, you're on the discard heap.

Seniority means "top of the list" in Congress (which happens to have, by the way, NO mandatory retirement age for itself, but cheerfully passes retirement laws affecting others)—in real life, "seniority" and "senility" mean about the same thing if you're over you-know-what.

Don't be so cheerful, America, as you portray us standing on a surfside beach with casting rod in hand, thrilled to death because we have no cares, no job, no one to be our boss. Paint the picture as it is, America. The agencies that you have spawned are now our boss. We have no jobs, that's true—you've seen to that, but friends, we do have cares. We also have an emptiness that you have caused by stamping null and void upon our future.

Here are some things you need to know, America!

We have strength, America.

And spirit, too.

We have energy, experience, and will to do.

We have know-how, skill, and knowledge.

We have perspective and a solid view of history.

WE made this country what it is today.

The only thing . . . along the way, we forgot about ourselves. And, thinking that the day would never come when we'd be in this fix, we did nothing to prevent the situation we now face. We watched it come, sure, but always it was coming for others, not us. It came slowly at first in the early years, then swifter in the mid-years, and now . . .

Slowly again.

For we are deprived of things to do which make time pass excitingly.

We are stalemated in our own lack of concern for self. We were too busy building this land for you.

And now, just look at us.

Obsolete . . .

In the way . . .

One-third of a whole country we are, and yet . . .

We're in the way . . .

Draining the reserves . . .

We're not the forgotten generation, that's for sure.

They are aware of us because we cost so much.

We cost so much because we aren't allowed to earn.

Dear Sir (or Madam as the case may be): We note that you earned a dollar-three-eighty-seven over your limit this month and therefore are not entitled to collect on your Social Security.

Social Security started out to be a way for folks to live in some aspect of pay-your-own-way dignity.

The folks who handle your "case" (remember you're not a person any longer, you're a "case") make it seem like dole.

Somehow a new philosophy grew up: "We obsolesce our products, why not do the same with humans?"

Since we built things to self-destruct when warranties ran out, why not solve the growing problem of the aging with such neat and orderly dispatch?

Of course, the "put-'em-on-an-ice-floe" theory wouldn't work, we're much too civilized for that, nor could we put them out of sight completely, so we built high-rise senior villages, geriatric parks, and homes away from home for those who hobbled, groaned, and ached. In this vicious cycle of "make it so it will wear out," materialism begat materialism and we were thrown away, a generation of us, all used up, all useless, our warranties run out, and now unneeded.

Maybe someday there'll be a sign we'll see which says: "Hertz Rent-a-Gramps. Great for family reunions and sentimental holidays."

Or maybe not.

Perhaps they'll find some for us after all.

But in the meanwhile . . .

We're angry, America, angry and disgusted.

We're tired of being discards, tired of being made to feel so useless, disgusted that you think that only "young" is beautiful and "old" is ugliness, tired of your forgetting it was us who made YOU, ashamed we didn't raise you to respect your elders more.

But wait around, America, and you'll be where we are now . . .

Decrepit . . .

Obsolete . . .

Good for nothing . . .
In the way . . .
You'll get there, America . . .
You'll be there by and by . . .
And then you'll be where we are now . . .
Unless, of course, you change it for the better.
Think of it, friends . . .
It won't be long 'till you are us . . .
And then you'll see!

Retirement for me was a totally different thing. I could hardly wait to retire. Anyone who has been president of a college for twenty years, including the 1960's, must welcome an honorable alternative. But I recognize how differently many people feel and how important it is to allow for individual freedom in anything as crucial as one's vocational life. About the most important thing that can be said about a person in America is his vocational identity. Scotland, with a Calvinistic background, regarded vocation as a divine call to each person. This was reflected in the Scottish custom of including the vocation along with the name inscribed on a gravestone. The cemetery at Dumfries, where Robert Burns lies buried, has this interesting characteristic. The dead are remembered for their vocations in such manner as Duncan MacTavish, Shipbuilder; Willie Duncan, Tailor; Robbie MacIntosh, Sailor; and Robert Burns, poet. Imagine a gravestone inscribed Robert MacNair, Thief.

When a person dies, this identification is lost. In a retirement community what a person has been yields little prestige. Those who have found personal dignity in a vocation may be genuinely diminished when that vocation is abruptly terminated. My lifelong friend B.E. Hutchinson, financial vice-president of the Chrysler Corporation, said "the sand runs out of man's bag quickly when he retires." Institutions and companies who undertake to encourage early retirement to accomplish their necessary purposes do well to find a civilized and humane way to deal with this traumatic problem which confronts some, if not many individuals.

INFLATION, THE ENEMY OF THE OLD

By all odds, the most horrendous threat to old people in America is inflation. The word is poorly understood by most people, even though it has a very simple origin. The word inflation refers to an increase in the money supply whether it be by printing press or credit. The result of increased supply is higher prices and wages. The reason governments all over the world turn to inflation is that they find it more palatable to increase the available money than to increase taxes when they need additional revenues to pay for expensive government projects, and they find it more to their advantage than to reduce government expenditures.

At one time, the amount of money governments could make available was limited by some kind of standard such as gold or silver. When these standards were abandoned, governments felt free, when pressed, to increase the money supply at will with absolutely ruinous consequences in some cases— such as Germany, Brazil and even France. Inflation is worldwide and has been going on for a long time. The rise in wages, for example, is dramatically shown by the Elizabethan nursery rhyme:

> "She shan't have but a penny a day
> Because she can't work any faster."

Since that period, prices and wages have risen consistently even though there were periods of deflation and falling prices. In my own boyhood, the standard wage for help on the ranch was a dollar a day, room and board. There was a common chuckle about the Irishman who was so pleased with his new wage of a dollar a day that he boasted, "If I work a million days, I'll have a million dollars!" Recent labor settlements in our community find some workers militantly refusing to reduce wages below $25 an hour, even though the company is in major distress. An increase of wages from a dollar a day to one hundred dollars a day in less than a century suggests the impact of inflation. Most of this impact has come in the recent past.

Inflation is the greatest enemy of old people because it is a thief that takes away the living earned by a lifetime of hard work. Economists have made the word "inflation" so complicated that many old people do not understand it even though they are robbed by it. What they do understand are the skyrocketing prices that inflation has brought about.

Not long ago, a retired couple could go out for dinner for less than ten dollars for a first-class meal, including refreshments and gratuities. Now the same couple may face a check of twenty-five dollars, or more than one hundred dollars in some places. A car that fairly recently cost four thousand dollars is now selling for eight to ten thousand dollars. A loaf of bread, which once cost ten or fifteen cents, is now pushing up toward seventy-five cents or a dollar.

Everyone understands the meaning of skyrocketing prices when one's hard-earned retirement income is frozen at a previous level. The retirement income that once meant a life of ease and plenty now means a life of poverty and anxiety.

It is time for those of us who are older to understand what powers these rising prices. The principal villain in all inflation is the government itself, since it is the sole source of the money supply. That money supply gets out of hand because the government needs more and more money to carry on more and more projects. Politicians are enamored of funding more money to pay for projects to assist or please people since this is the way for a politician to get votes when running for public office. Bureaucrats are eager to increase their position and power by developing larger and larger organizations to carry on bigger and more exciting programs.

When an uncontrollable catastrophe such as a war comes along, inflation simply goes wild. Prices and wages rise, and the people in government, for very good reasons from their standpoint, do not let them come down when the war is over. People in business and industry likewise look with disfavor on falling prices. Nobody likes to see his wage reduced. One round of inflation follows another and all of us are robbed.

I do not say that the government is the sole cause of rising prices. I am not unaware of the influence of cartels as the dramatic price increases imposed on oil by the OPEC nations have shown. I am not unaware of the similar impact by the coffee-producing countries and by the cartel price-rises of sugar. I know that those involved in a monopoly situation will try to use it to their own advantage—whether it be an industry, an association, a labor union or a corporation. We are the culprits because everybody wants inflation for himself but not for anybody else. The government, however, is the principal factor in the price rises that rob the old.

The dollar today will purchase less than half what it would have ten years ago. All of us are going broke at an alarming rate of speed.

I feel sick at heart when I hear my friends talk about bringing inflation down to six or seven per cent. Think of an old person with his money in a savings bank—losing one or two per cent of his capital every year. The purchasing power of his money has fallen below his original investment.

Adding to the problem of rising prices is the additional problem of increasing taxes. Rising prices and increasing taxes are the jaws of the vise in which all of us are caught. These taxes rise because special-interest groups ask more and more from government.

Allan Meltzer, a cherished colleague who teaches economics at Carnegie Mellon University, has pointed out that governments grow because benefits are concentrated and costs are diffused. This is a brilliant way of saying that when some special-interest group, such as those of us in education, ask for a government subsidy, the subsidy means a lot to us but does not cost anybody very much when it is spread over the entire nation. The people who have no interest in education are not inspired to mobilize against the program. When those of us who are in education push hard enough, everybody else goes along and we have an additional government program.

Everybody gets into the same kind of act. Depressed industry demands help; safety crusaders demand support, the military requires more and more of those of us who are older get into the act with a series of new requests. Layer after layer of government bureaucracy is added and the costs of government build to the point where more and more taxes must be levied. Even this will not suffice, and the money supply is increased to cover the expense of new projects not covered by tax revenues, with the result that the vice squeezes the old person until he is forced onto welfare. This, in turn, increases the burgeoning costs of government.

What can we do about this vicious situation? The answer is that we can mobilize for less government instead of more, for fewer taxes instead of more benefits. There is a rising revolt against the taxes that are robbing old people of their homes. Everywhere a person turns, he is taxed: he pays sales tax, he pays a tax on gasoline and any number of specific items, he is taxed on most services, taxed at the theatre, taxed at the restaurant, taxed at the hotel. He pays tax on his property, tax on his travel, tax on his income, which may be almost confiscatory to many old people. In most places he pays state income tax and sometimes local income tax in addition. It is time for us to let the world know that there can be no "goodies" from the government without taxes that come out of the hides of the people.

Many of us are enchanted today with such expensive government programs as come to us from those crusaders who want to protect the environment, the consumers, the minorities, the schools, the cities, the railroads and all of the many services that are proclaimed as highly useful and required of any socially responsible nation. Many of these are good and necessary, but some of them we must learn to do ourselves rather than create expensive government bureaucracies that will drive people into ruin and poverty in the next few years unless some remedy is found.

Old people, better than anyone else, should know that somebody has to pay into the government before the government can pay anything out to anybody.

There are other things that old people can do to fight inflation and to deal with sky-rocketing prices that result from it. We can individually become more astute in our purchasing. We can, if pressed, find ways to develop many of our own resources, like the several communities of older Americans who have developed their own sources of food supplies and discount stores for things they must purchase. They have learned how to travel at greatly reduced costs. Old people are better able to live resourcefully and by their wits than are many younger people who have less experience and less compelling motive of necessity.

The great challenge for those of us who are past middle age, however, is that we bring some kind of compelling influence to bear against our enemy, which is inflation. Since government is the principal factor involved, we must let our politicians know that we need less government instead of more, less intervention and less meddling in our lives. We can no longer afford the luxury of being taxed to death on the one hand and inflated to death on the other. We do not look with favor on becoming destitute wards of the state when we know that the state itself is on the way to bankruptcy.

We seem to have no satisfactory alternative to an all-out fight against inflation. The best people in the government itself realize the predicament and may even help our cause.

CRIME

Those of us who are growing old in America are easy targets for the criminal element. Almost every metropolitan daily carries the story of robberies, bilking, beatings and muggings of old people. Some young punks make a living snatching purses from little old ladies.

When I was young, I heard of an occasional crime against an older person but not often. Now, I can think of more than a dozen friends who have been victimized by criminals, some of them badly injured. We need protection.

Even the most ardent advocate of limited government assumes that defense of the realm and police protection are fundamental roles for government. In the sixties we lived through a time when rights of offenders received more public attention and so-called "compassionate concern" than the rights of old people who need protection from wanton and preventable crime.

Those of us who are older might do well to press for reparation by government when we are victims of crime. We have organized government and paid taxes to protect us from these outrageous events to which we are exposed. Anyone who has been mugged, robbed, beaten or raped will find it hard to pity and set free the perpetrator just because he is disadvantaged or young. Revenge is not our motive, but reparation for the damage and penalty for the crime should be our objective. We must lift our voices with regard to the fact that the very governments established to protect us have, through their courts and systems of justice, returned to the streets those who have robbed us, so that they can rob again.

Everybody has a stake in crime prevention, but older people have a particular interest because they are more often the victims. I do not presume to speak for anyone else, but I for one would much prefer public expenditures to prevent crime than public expenditures to tell me what I should eat, what I should do with my time, how much I can earn—and a thousand other paternalistic services which sometimes, if not often, do no good and occasionally do great harm.

If I could speak to the appropriate people in the government in behalf of my contemporaries, I would say: Treat us with respect, give us an opportunity to work and to learn, protect us from crime and, beyond that, reduce public expenditures and pursue monetary policies that will reduce inflation. The things we lose to criminals are nothing in comparison to the amount we lose when we are robbed by our own government. Inflation is an insidious form of robbery. Anyone who has seen his fixed income dwindle at such a rate as to threaten his livelihood has most certainly been robbed.

MAKE YOUR OWN CLIMATE

I contend that the social and political climate in America is not fair to the aging. This does not imply that the aging fare any better in Western Europe. For the most part, they are much worse off. There are some cultures where old people are venerated, but this, too, is a distortion of justice.

All of us should rise above the difficulties that confront old people today and make something of the rest of our lives. There are aging people who earn enough and invest wisely enough to outrun inflation; people who are strong enough to overcome all the stereotypes, people who are public-spirited enough to exercise some influence on public opinion, people who have put the lie to those who say "Old people can't do anything." All around us are people who have experienced the surge of the sixties and who are having the best time of their lives.

It is much easier to sit around and complain than it is to perform. Anybody who lives in America has sufficient liberty to make something of his own life. Retired people have the best opportunity of all. They can continue to learn and disprove a stereotype but, even more, they can enjoy the thrill of discovery. They can create poetry, music, sculpture, history, axhandles, jigsaw puzzles, gardens, cuisine, clothing, gadgets and a whole multitude of things that bring profit as well as joy. We all differ in talent. Some are best fitted to lead while others prefer to be good followers. Both are important.

Older people have an opportunity to exercise true leadership in government, community, religion and secular affairs. There is no time like now for an aging person to make his life count for something. Old age is not merely golden years, but golden opportunity.

This very day brings the greatest opportunity in history for those of us who really care about the quality of life for older people in America. We have all the information accumulated by hundreds of old-age studies throughout the world. We have new political techniques to organize and exercise our influence. We stand face to face with the major problem of inflation while our government officials talk about it, but make it worse by increasing government expenditures.

Howard Jarvis has shown us what can be done by those who resent being taxed out of their very existence. We can mobilize our political clout against conditions that allow criminals to prey upon the old. We can organize to influence public opinion toward reducing government interference in our lives. We can finally get the kind of government we deserve.

NOT IF I CAN HELP IT

A renewed person past sixty is about the most admirable person in the whole range of the human generations. The sixties, the seventies and beyond are the years of wisdom, integrity, serenity and peace. Some, to be sure, miss their opportunities for renewal and go doggedly on without happiness, joy or achievement. They have somehow failed to wait upon the Lord.

Life is not easy to manage at any age. Teenagers have a terrible time finding out who they are. Young families are always in a dither. Men and women at the apex of their vocational careers are often overburdened with stress.

The natural glory of a person in the "golden years" depends not only on the boundless power of God, but on his own performance. He must manage his life if he is to receive the strength to "mount up with wings as eagles." Renewal will be of little value unless he can develop the quality and style of life that goes with his personal intelligence and integrity.

There are things to avoid as well as things to do if a person wishes to make the most of his renewed life. Here are a few observations I feel warranted to make after close observation of a few of my contemporaries. I do not wish to be critical of any of my colleagues. I realize that each of us has his own set of problems. And my idiosyncrasies may seem more obnoxious to my friends than some of theirs do to me. The following series of resolutions, however, may suggest even better lists for my readers.

Browning was only fifty-two when he wrote, "Grow old along with me," but he had the good sense to trust the testimony of Rabbi Ben Ezra, who was a celebrated septuagenarian scholar. I am just now seventy and I trust the testimony of my many friends, especially my old friend, Edgar DeWitt Jones, prominent Detroit clergyman and newspaper columnist, who said most eloquently, "Life begins at seventy!"

In preparation for the decade following these three score years and ten, I have made certain resolutions. I was even more excited about my seventieth birthday than I was at eighteen about my twenty-first. I hope to live up to the high standards set for me by friends like Andy Holt, President Emeritus of the University of Tennessee, and W.E. Garrison, literary critic and Professor of History at the University of Chicago; but I hope even more to avoid mistakes made by many who have preceded me into the enchanting years. Rabbi Ben Ezra held before us the intriguing promise: "The best is yet to be!" Some, however, have performed in such a manner that the luster of these years has been tarnished if not removed.

I shall, with the help of God, my family, and friends, restrain my tongue—even though I have been a teacher, lecturer, preacher, speaker and opinionater throughout my professional life. Some old people suffer from incontinence of various kinds, but the most commonly obvious is not knowing when to shut up. I have heard ceaseless monologues from an old friend I have visited with the hope that I might share some important information and receive some from him in return. He regales me with trivia which have fleeting interest for him, but absolutely none for me.

Friends who knew the late Franklin D. Roosevelt well say he was a monologist in his declining years.

Oliver Wendell Holmes is reputed to have been an excellent conversationalist and listener right up to the end of his ninety-four years. His celebrated father reached only the age of eighty-six, but he was at his witty best in his last decade.

I resolve to speak when the occasion calls for it and to listen when the occasion indicates silence. I want to converse truly with people—not just suffer them to speak while I plan my next remark.

I am determined not to brag. Advancing years dull the senses and shake the ego. A threatened ego may turn to glorified accounts of mighty deeds performed in years gone by—this is a sort of defense against the inevitable loss of powers and the loss of status which follows.

Some of my friends who are well into their seventies are the most amazing braggarts. The romantic achievements of an ordinary youth have been embellished and improved by a strong desire and a slipping memory until yesterday's dullard sounds like an irresistible Lothario. A miserable war record comes out as the greatest military accomplishment since Horatio stood at the bridge. Pride in travel may turn otherwise attractive people into boasting bores. Every man is a hero to himself, but he must remember that he is just one more person to everybody else.

Recollections of a good solid vocational career may be of some benefit to a person who needs reassurance of his value to the world, but even that great celebrity Ty Cobb once told me that he regretted the baseball career which kept him from entering the field of medicine, as he had once intended. The aging survivor of the Wright brothers must have grown weary of recounting Kitty Hawk, but his weariness was nothing in comparison to that of those who had to listen.

I hope to savor the past from time to time, but my present worth must provide its own essence. Faded laurels are less than fragrant.

I intend to wear my glasses when I shave. Small thickets of grey whiskers here and there are unsightly and unnecessary. Some of my most illustrious contemporaries have the appearance of a bedraggled bird in moulting season. Most seniors have sufficiently impaired vision to make them totally unaware of the skips and oversights in the shaving routine.

I hope I can always count on the benevolent service of an honest *sniffer* who loves me enough to tell the painful truth. Even the most meticulous of the older set becomes inured to the various odors that are associated with the person. Who can smell his own breath or be aware of his own body odors? Booze, garlic, or onions may diminish an otherwise charming personality. Clothing which reeks of cigars, horses, dogs, cats, sweat or mothballs does an old man no good in the eye of friend and contemporary.

As the acuity of vision and hearing diminish, the need for a frank and friendly *inspector* is enhanced. The old man with egg on his face and gravy on his necktie is less to blame for such apparent carelessness than are the members of his household who have protected his pride but left him exposed to unfavorable comment. A trustworthy inspector can mention wrinkles, the button, the zipper and the clashing colors as well as the smudges and the water spots. The *helpful listener* can mention the hummings, the throat clearings, the wheezes, the rumblings and other sounds of the elderly which might escape the man who hears less well than he used to. Even squeaky shoes can get by undetected unless there is a listener in the house. I have stopped, looked, and listened for my friends—now they can do as much for me!

Too many old people resent being helped. *I have sworn my intention to thank God and my family for sniffing, inspecting, listening, advising and otherwise helping me to avoid the common pitfalls.* When some member of my family or some friend oversteps the bounds of propriety, however, and tries to manage my life, I shall express my gratitude for help in the areas where I need it, but I shall reaffirm my intention to live my own life. Those who are close enough to know my needs are close enough to know my proud independence.

At a much more serious level, *I pledge my firm intention not to withdraw from the continuing drama of life,* which is in need of some veterans to bring off a credible play. Old people who just sit and rock have dozed through their greatest opportunities. The harvest of experience in work, play, love, and worship is of major importance to the audience as well as to the players.

Benjamin Franklin was at his best in the eighties, and Howard Jarvis brought off the California tax revolt when he was pressing on toward seventy. Rabbi Ben Ezra was right when he called on us to enjoy "the last of life for which the first was made."

I have promised myself that *I shall live my renewed life without the stupid pretense that I am still young.* I cannot run as fast as I once did; I cannot recall as quickly as was my pride in college days; I cannot endure the sustained pace which marked my middle years. *Yet* I am in fine health and able to do some things better than I could manage in my youth. The sensible attitude is full enjoyment of a renewed life along *with honest admission of the delightful process of aging.*

Take romantic love, for instance. Mature love can be more tender than fierce young love. Wine labeled "spatlese" indicates grapes of the late harvest as more cherished than the first fruits of spring. Love lasts as long as life, but some of its expressions need modification as befits the time of wisdom and integrity. The peace of mind that comes from diminished sexual passion may bring happiness and relief to many who have reached the ninety years of Cephalus in Plato's *Republic.* Each person must find the way of life that brings personal satisfaction and fulfillment. Many renewed people find joy and delight in romantic love, even when they are in the nineties!

Age has vocational implications. The idea that a man must hold on to his position until he is carried out in a box belongs to the days of the plow, the ax, and the rifle. A change in one's vocation may be a good thing for some or even many. The very act of retiring from one post may mean even more fulfillment. Let me not resemble the man who was described as having all the Christian virtues except that of resignation. *Let me live life to the full in work, play and service; but let me never forget that renewal and change are also part of life.* Continuity is not the only value; balance may be better than stubborn persistence.

Memory may diminish with age; quick recall may become more difficult. I have begun to develop crutches to help me remember and to keep me from asking the same questions over and over again. As an old college professor, I have every right to be absentminded, and I have very well illustrated the stereotype from my youth. But the memory blocks brought on by possible accidents or sclerosis of the blood vessels is a much more serious problem. When my mind is merely distracted by more interesting thoughts, I can clear it and meet the issue. When recall falters, I must find some way to compensate for my handicap. A few legible notes are a great help. I can anticipate my needs and prepare by writing down the facts and figures that may be required. I have learned that some deliberate attention to things I wish to remember can be of considerable benefit.

Concentration is just a little bit more important at seventy or eighty than it is at forty. I have friends who are well past fourscore years who show no diminution of power to recall and remember. After careful inquiry, I have concluded that deliberate concentration has helped them as much as their natural resistance to aging. A good clean set of arteries is the best assistance, but a clogged set can be partially accommodated by resourceful attention.

A really good memory course can do just as much for an old man as a really good golf lesson or a dancing lesson. Mental exercise is just as possible as physical exercise. Performance can be improved by diligent practice in either case. Aids to memory by association and other such devices may be as useful to the old as to the young—and may be much more needed! Repetition at convenient intervals will fix words, sentences, and ideas in the mind and thereby facilitate recall when the moment arrives. Memory gymnastics for the seventies and eighties may sound like nonsense to some; but *I have resolved to hold on to my memory as long as possible,* and I believe exercise is the best way to do it. Sir Isaac Newton was right when he said, "Attending the mind to it is the best solution of any problem."

I realize that people become more and more like themselves as they grow older. *I have begun to meet this problem by attempting to accentuate the positive.* I have enough self-insight and enough experience to know pretty well what patterns of behavior and speech are most acceptable—and which are most objectionable!

The practice of kindness and consideration for the other person is even more appealing in advancing years. Kind and gentle old people are about the most admirable old people in the world. A young ingrate is unpleasant, but an old one is insufferable. Brutal candor and sharp tongue can be condoned, even admired in the salty old man, but raffishness and surliness—never!

I am determined to be sensitive to the needs and interests of other people. Some of my contemporaries go through the golden years with the approximate awareness of a lost puppy in an art gallery. The old man who notices, cares, and shows consideration is both loved and happy. Some old men overdo their attentions to other people and become obnoxious, but the vast majority of aging humans suffer from self-centered myopia. The Golden Rule is the perfect guide to the golden years!

I here and now promise all gentle people with whom I am associated that *I shall not become an opinionated, unreasonable, stubborn old bullhead.* One of my former friends in his eightieth year presumed to know more about higher education than all of the dedicated people who were both trained and experienced in the field. This old man was a former engineer whose only knowledge of colleges came from his course in engineering almost sixty years before! Hardened attitudes can be more damaging than hardened arteries, but the two seem to go together.

Old people who try to play God usually play the Devil instead! Benjamin Franklin decided to practice humility for a week. He made careful notes of his performance only to discover that he was "much less virtuous than he had supposed." Arrogance seems to come naturally to the senior active members of society. *I shall remember the wise counsel of John Calvin, who said, "The three great words of the Christian Religion are humility, humility, and humility!"*

I intend to keep busy at important work as long as I live. Retirement brings an opportunity to work at some enterprises long neglected because of heavy vocational demands. One of my academic colleagues took early retirement to become a successful and happy insurance executive. My friend Frank Sparks closed his brilliant career in business to become a college president. He then retired in time to set up a national program for the support of all private higher education. Any second career may be more fun than the first one—especially if it has a great deal of meaning for humanity. A decent old man likes to be of service to his fellows, and a second career is a good way to do it.

When the time comes to retire from the second or third career, there is always another—performance of public service functions which have meaning and require capable people who can afford the time and money involved. I refer to hospitals, churches, schools, political parties, societies and a host of others that are always in need of help.

Since my retirement as a college president, I have served on the boards of several business corporations, lectured, written for fun and for profit, taught in faraway places such as Athens and Glasgow, improved my golf and given my time to several public service institutions. Every year brings new interests and opportunities for service. I have been able to strike my best blows for individual liberty and to give my best witness to the spiritual, moral, and intellectual causes that have concerned me throughout a long professional career in higher education and religion. As the years accumulate, my role changes and my activities are modified to fit my abilities to the various tasks which need doing. I shall be hard at work when the sun goes down.

I shall play more than I have before, but I shall not try to make up for seventy years of neglect in the comparatively short time I have left. Some of my friends kill themselves at golf, boating, bridge, shuffleboard, travel, tennis, jogging, swimming, or horses with just the same fierce competition with which they formerly punished themselves at work. The line between work and play is one of attitude. Any activity can become work, providing little or no fun, and any wholesome and honorable work can become fun. It all depends on the worker and the player. I intend to work hard when I work, play hard when I play, and throw myself into the game of life with abandon; *but never will I let myself become obsessed* to the point that I am like Captain Ahab in pursuit of the great white whale. The Aristotelian golden mean is for the golden years quite as much as is the golden rule!

I shall never willingly retire my mind. Spectacles and reading glasses will keep books open for me even when my vision becomes impaired. Electronic devices will continue to bring me news from the Rialto and the more venerable reflections of philosophy. Even if I should become both blind and deaf, I could still think about and discuss the problems of humanity.

I may enjoy nostalgic television shows along with my oldtimer friends, but I shall pitch my conversation at a more substantive level than sports and television. Even now, I find some of my contemporaries hesitant to talk about the state of the world, the nature of the universe and the predicament of modern man. A person is sometimes afraid to initiate any kind of intellectual conversation lest he be regarded as a show-off. Banal talk is not new, nor is it limited to the mature set. Schopenhauer placed a guinea on the lunch table each day as a bet with himself that the men would discuss nothing but women and sports. Not once did he have to leave the money on the table for the waiter.

Control of one's own resources is of prime importance to the practice of renewal in the sixties, seventies and thereafter. *I intend to keep control of my money, my pursuits, my place of residence and my priorities for as long as it is feasible to do so.* The tragedy of my aging friends who have given their money away to their relatives or to some institution, only to find themselves dependent and even resented, gives me pause. The person who is uprooted from home and friends just to please his children or to follow the advice of well-meaning friends may rue the day. To be general manager of one's own life is not only a high responsibility but a high privilege. When feebleness and infirmity require that I turn over my affairs to someone else, I shall do so as graciously as possible, but I have no intention of losing control when the time has not yet come.

Observation and experience tell me that loneliness is a major problem for the aging. Everyone feels lonely on occasion, and some are forever disturbed by feelings of isolation, but *feelings of loneliness appear to be more intense and more frequent with age.* Infinite longings for people that were dear and for days that are gone sweep over the pilgrims of advanced journeys. *When such feelings come, as come they may, I shall go to work, play some golf, take a walk, write a poem, or call a friend.*

The vague feelings of loneliness derive from helplessness and loss of powers. Nobody, however, is completely helpless, and everybody has more powers than he utilizes. Renewal awaits the expectant heart. *I shall practice the art of friendship more assiduously as the years wear on.* To love and to be loved are the greatest values to anybody—especially to those of us who are septuagenarians, octogenarians and even nonagenarians.

Enthusiasm, courage, optimism and zest for life are the traits of a veteran who has learned how to live and provide some enjoyment for those around him. Confucious once said, "The sin of youth is lust; the sin of middle age is struggle; but the sin of old age is avarice." I know many oldsters who have bucked the trend. People of good will who know how to live, love, think truth and trust God are always in demand. The person who exemplifies such civil and humane values as gratitude, loyalty, compassion and generosity is immortal. He is like wine and violins, which get better with aging. I hope to be that kind of person and prove that for me, at least, life begins at seventy—or maybe eighty!

The person who manages to avoid the pitfalls of aging has an enhanced opportunity for the periodic renewals that come to many in later years. Self-discipline is an essential ingredient for the realization of opportunity. I can manage to stay alert to the challenges of each new day and avoid the restrictive and hampering habits and inclinations in accordance with my resolutions. I confidently expect my closing decades to fulfill the promise of Rabbi Ben Ezra. I here and now invite every person who has reached that magic age of seventy to join in the fun!

THE IMAGES OF AGING

Every thoughtful person has a philosophy of
life, whether he knows it or not. The assumptions which underlie this philosophy derive, in part,
from thoughts, feelings and values developed in
early youth. Standards of right and wrong, appropriate and inappropriate, good and bad, are not only a part of every society but are part of the belief
and value system of each of us. A person's values
result in the vision, the expectations and the manner in which his life is conducted. An older person
who has an image of age as a painful necessity and
as a penalty for having been born will go his melancholy way until death claims him. Those whose
values and beliefs give them the expectation of
vibrant and renewed years tend to realize their expectations and, in so doing, live a life of joy.

The vibrant human organism attempting to renew a doleful and pessimistic life will utterly fail.
Great new surges of energy pass by unnoticed for

the cynical and resigned pessimist. The person with the expectant heart, however, will be able to "mount up with wings as eagles."

I want here to outline three images of aging. In oversimplified terms, they are: 1) life as an obsolescent machine; 2) life as a biological cycle, and 3) life as a series of renewals. For purposes of brevity, I have called them the old-car theory, the old-tree theory, and the eagle-wing theory.

These images of aging have been present throughout all human history. The materialistic mechanical theory was predominant with the ancient Egyptians when they were building the pyramids. Materialism characterized some of the ancient Chinese when they were in the gray dawn of our civilization. The organic-cycle theory existed alongside the mechanical theory and became the theme for ancient mythology, identifying human life with the changing seasons. The mystery cults were built around the death of the flowers in autumn and their renascence in spring. The renewal theory, however, was more hinted at than expounded, more exemplified than proclaimed.

I am deliberately avoiding the important studies in the field of gerontology dealing with the genetics of life, which may some day conclude that senility is a curable disease. I have many biologist friends who firmly believe with Bernard L. Strehler that even death may be overcome by our scientific advances. Albert Rosenfeld, who reports these new studies in his book *Pro-Longevity*, concludes:

> Running contrapuntally through all theories of aging are a pair of controversial themes, either of which is in harmony with most of the observed facts. One holds that damage to the genetic machinery or errors in the protein-

making process are the result of accident and incident, of wear and tear. The competing view, as we know, holds that most of the damage and errors expressed in the aging cell are dictated by the genes themselves, the on-off switches bringing *new* genes into play which start dismantling or disrupting the protein assembly lines so that the organism runs down by explicit program. In the latter case—with life and its demise all part of a single genetic package—if we could control the DNA, all the DNA, then we should be able to keep those assembly lines moving. Maybe not forever, but for an impressively long time.[1]

I am greatly impressed with the studies that are going on, but they are not essential to an understanding of these three major images of aging. As an old professor, I am mainly interested in reporting what I have found by personal experience, careful observation, and a life-long study of philosophy. Thus, I am narrowing the parameters of the chapter even though I look forward to any scientific advances as much as my most optimistic friends.

THE OLD-CAR IMAGE

I have called this the old-car theory because most people have firsthand knowledge of an automobile wearing out. It does not fall apart all at once, but breaks down in various places. The tires are damaged, the battery fails, the front wheels wobble, the transmission wears out, the spark plugs get dirty, the shock absorbers break. These mechanical interruptions are repaired one at a time, but the car goes on to a time when it is beyond repair and winds up on the scrap heap. The occasional car becomes a

---

1 Rosenfeld, Albert, *Pro-Longevity* (New York: Alfred A. Knopf, Inc. 1976), p. 29.

classic, but it endures to that ripe old age only because it has had unusual care and constant repair. It is never truly renewed; it is still a machine with some repaired parts.

Long before there were automobiles, however, people thought of the body in mechanical and materialistic terms. This philosophy assumes that the old body is certain to wear out and that the inconvenience and suffering of old age may be somewhat reduced by diligent care in an effort to keep it functioning as long as possible. The old-car theory holds out no hope and encourages no expectation of anything better.

Many sophisticated physicians, psychologists, biologists and gerontologists are influenced by this mechanical analogy. Edward J. Stieglitz, for instance, raises the question of whether we wear out or rust out.[2]

His language embodies the old-car theory.

In either case, the body is a machine and the only question is how it is best cared for: Is it better to use it at full speed and wear it out, or to protect it and let it rust out? Many contemporary physicians have accepted this physical inevitability, essentially mechanical in nature. There are surgeons who remove or repair organs on the assumption that the process is purely mechanical. There are internists who fit the chemistry of medicine to the mechanical body to improve its function. There are even theologians who think of human beings as God-created

---

2 Steiglitz, "The Personal Challenge of Aging," *Living Through the Older Years*, ed. Clark Tibbetts (Ann Arbor: University of Michigan Press, 1944), p. 53.

souls living in mechanical bodies. Even science-fiction writers have created bionic people who puzzle the old and fascinate the young.

Empedocles introduced two unusual factors which he called Love and Hate. This colorful genius of ancient Greece described the material world in terms of earth, air, fire and water—all influenced by the evolutionary forces of Love which combines, and Hate which dissipates.

Physician as well as poet, statesman as well as philosopher, Empedocles wore golden sandals and played the role of a god. As age came on, according to legend, he withdrew from his earlier materialism and became more and more of a prophet. Having played god for so many years, he could not bring himself to admit mortality—especially in the presence of his worshippers. He donned his divine robes and golden sandals, stood on the crater's edge at Mount Etna and threw himself into the cauldron. The bubbling lava regurgitated the golden slippers and threw them out upon the lip of the crater. Thus, as the legend goes, his pretense to immortality was foiled. The discovered slippers were mute testimony to his earlier materialism as well as to his mortality.

Democritus, however, was the great high priest of materialism. He denied the reality of human conventions such as color, taste, sound, and temperature. For him reality was nothing but "atoms and the void." Human beings, he argued, are combinations of various atoms moving around in space. As is the case with most philosophers of mechanistic materialism, his life transcended his thought. He lived to the ripe old age of one hundred nine. Using his logic I must say that his mental atoms must have practiced such virtues as culture and moderation so effectively that his muscle and bone atoms lasted a long time. He was the old car that became a classic. He closed his life by eating less and less until he starved to death. All this was four centuries before Christ.

These early philosophers sound naive but were, in fact, rather sophisticated in describing the mechanical and materialistic theory of human life. In our own time, a famous physiologist, Dr. Anton Julius Carlson of the University of Chicago, elaborated this sophisticated mechanical theory in modern scientific terms. His students nicknamed him "Ajax."

I shall forever remember a debate between the famous nuclear physicist Arthur Compton and the celebrated Ajax Carlson during the early 1930's. Dr. Carlson argued that man is a mechanism just as much as any old car, with all of his actions determined by stimulus and response. For him the cells of the human body were a machine. The freedom of choice, said Carlson, is purely specious. A person may imagine that he prefers to fish on his day off, but some event has stimulated this desire, and his action results from the mechanical stimulus rather than from any genuine preference.

Dr. Compton, on the other hand, argued for freedom of the human will, basing this upon his theory of the random behavior which he had observed in the molecules that form the human organism. It was a fascinating debate. The same argument had been made by Democritus and Heraclitus long before there was any science of physiology or physics, and very long before there was any understanding of nuclear behavior.

Many of the people who make up my circle of friends assume this mechanical image of aging. Anyone wishing to compliment me says, "You look young." This assumes that if I look my age, I am about to wear out. People expect those who are aging to act old—they say, "Act your age." Their implication is that a person starts out as a new piece of machinery and wears out a little at a time until he is ready for the junk heap. Old cars should not be driven as fast as new cars. I play golf with a wonderful friend who describes the late seventies as "just waiting for the undertaker." While he is waiting, he always manages to beat me at golf. I cannot get him to see that the human organism renews itself, or that, in biblical terms, if he would wait on the Lord instead of the undertaker, he might be renewed.

Except for the theoretical people like Democritus or Ajax Carlson, most of my friends recognize that a human being is more than a piece of machinery. They cannot escape, however, from the old-car image of aging. When they talk seriously about getting the most out of life, they fall back on the formula, "Stay young as long as you can." They have completely missed the possibility of renewal. The colorful American poet Vachel Lindsay took a dim view of this mechanical conception of a human being and wrote a clever little verse which is more effective, in my opinion, than a careful scientific argument for freedom of the human will:

There's machinery in the butterfly,
There's a mainspring to the bee.
There's hydraulics to a daisy
And contraptions to a tree.

69

If we could see the birdie
That makes the chirping sound
With psycho-analytic eyes,
With X-ray, scientific eyes,
We could see the wheels go round.

And I hope all men
Who think like this
Will soon lie underground.

THE OLD-TREE IMAGE

Greeks, Indians and Chinese in the ancient world looked on human life as vegetation which springs up, matures, grows old and dies as the seasons turn. Some of the mystery religions dramatize a picture of youth in the springtime, maturity in summer, old age in autumn, and death in winter.

The story of Persephone, daughter of Demeter and Zeus, captured by Hades when she was gathering the flowers of summer, is a mythical account of this cyclical life view which was popular in ancient Greece. Hades spirited his fair captive down to the netherworld, where she reigned as queen.

Demeter called Helios to help find her daughter. At last, with the aid of the sun god she found Persephone reigning in the realms of darkness. Demeter hurried to Zeus and implored him to help her recover the beautiful girl. Zeus said he could help only if Persephone had not eaten anything while she was Hades' captive queen. Alas for Demeter, Persephone had eaten a few seeds from a pomegranate. A compromise, however, was worked out between Demeter and Hades whereby Persephone could be free except for the few months when she was to return to Hades as a penalty for having eaten the seeds. The beautiful Persephone returned to the hills and vales of Hellas. As she walked along, spring came to that storied land. Each place she stepped brought forth a trailing arbutus. As autumn came, time drew near for her to return to Hades. The vegetation took on the colors of age and prepared for the long winter of her absence. So ends the mythical image of the life cycle.

The old-tree image of aging is far more sophisticated than this beautiful Greek myth might indicate. Charles Darwin, for example, wrote his book *The Origin of Species* on the assumption that biological survival is the principal function of a human being. Many contemporary biologists and physiologists assume that survival of the race is the principal function of each individual. People are born, grow to maturity, beget and bear young to replenish the race, then grow old and die just as do old animals, old trees and all other living things.

Organic determinism is no less fatalistic than mechanical determinism. Human life appears in terms of the life cycle lived out in nature. The amazing salmon, for example, dares the rapids with incredible courage and unbelievable instinct. With heroic bursts of energy, males and females alike batter themselves as they drive blindly upstream to the quiet waters where they spawn and die. Lifeless forms of once brave fish wash down the river or disintegrate in the mountain sand. Some poetic writers are able to make the old-tree image of aging appear as something very beautiful. The twelfth chapter of Ecclesiastes is a prime example. The cycle of life becomes a work of art in this venerable poem.

The fact that many people are content with the old-tree theory explains the feelings that possess some mothers who feel useless and unhappy when their children are grown. They are acting out the biological, cyclical image of old age and death following reproduction. They have come to expect that they will wither and die as do the salmon, the beautiful flowers of summer and the stout old oak trees which endure for a few centuries before they come down in some ill-fated wind or die from their inability to ward off predatory insects and diseases.

The masculine fear of losing reproductive power may be related to this assumption that a person is primarily born to replenish the race. The tragedy of such a vision of life is that a person who thinks of his function as disintegration and death after the period of parenthood is likely to fulfill his expectation. Nothing could be more unfortunate in human history than for mankind to be deprived of the service, wisdom, beauty and influence of older people who have earned some freedom from the responsibilities of parenthood and vocational life.

It is not the function of the old to disintegrate and die. It is their function to live and serve with joy.

What is the origin of the old-tree theory? Oriental philosophies and religions are likely sources of our cyclical images of aging. Hinduism, for example, openly worships Shiva, the God of Destruction. Kali, feminine consort of Shiva, was the principal deity of many common people in ancient India. This terrible goddess was portrayed in black with her mouth open and tongue protruding. She was adorned with snakes, skulls and miniature dead men as she danced upon a corpse. Her face and breasts were smeared with blood. This frank declaration of decay and death as facts of life inspired the worshippers to reproduction in order to maintain the race. The Hindu trinity contained not only Shiva the Destroyer, but also Brahma the Creator and Vishnu the Preserver. Aging was looked upon as the penalty for having been born. Reincarnation continued the cycle of birth, growth, reproduction and death. The vegetational analogy was complete. People are like trees that sprout, grow, wither, decay and die, only to reappear in other trees or other forms.

Leaving his wife and son, Buddha became a celibate monk after he had seen an old man, a sick man and a dead man. As he identified with each of the three, his life changed. He went forth to find defense against the evils of sickness, decay and death. Throughout his long life Buddha looked upon pain and death as so out of proportion to pleasure in life that he considered it fortunate not to be born. The noble ethical and moral system which bears his name is a tribute to the self-denial and integrity of this remarkable person. Many of the most cherished doctrines of Judaism and Christianity appear in the more primitive teachings of Buddha. He lived to be eighty, honoring all the while his Five Moral Rules:

1. Let not one kill any living thing.
2. Let not one take what is not given to him.
3. Let not one speak falsely.
4. Let not one drink intoxicating drinks.
5. Let not one be unchaste.

His last words to his monks were: "Subject to decay are compound things. Strive with earnestness." But the beauty and power of his own later years are the best refutation of his pessimistic image of aging.

The Chinese image of aging was much more optimistic than that of India. Wise old people were honored and even venerated at the time of Confucius. A culture which honored wisdom could hardly ignore older people, for long experience and disciplined attitudes tend toward wisdom. Confucius was more successful as a wise man than as a statesman, even though he held high office in several Chinese states. As he came up to the end of his life, he was somewhat disturbed by the fact that he had been unable to bring his government to order and righteousness.

The ancient Chinese, like us, found virtue more difficult to espouse than to praise. They could tolerate the lofty doctrines of the old Master, but they drew back from placing him in a position of power. Confucius comforted one of his pupils, who felt similar neglect, with the wise admonition: "Do not worry about not holding high position; worry rather about playing your proper role. Worry not that no one knows of you; seek to be worth knowing."

The surge of the sixties must have given Confucius a new incentive to teach and sufficient energy to do it well, for he was more highly regarded when he was in his seventies than when he was at the height of his political power in the early fifties. He died at seventy-two. His followers mourned him for three years. The wise old Master accepted the cyclical image of aging but nevertheless exemplified the renewal which comes to those who wait upon the Lord.

The old-tree image of aging is probably the most widely held even today. Those of us who have pets see them grow old and die. We assume that something similar will happen to us one day. We hear songs about September and we see our own lives in terms of fading summer. The poets write about life's autumn leaves and we find ourselves emotionally involved in approaching winter. We speak of grey hair as snowy and we compare our wrinkles to dried fruit. Such terms as "the golden years" have reference to both yellow leaves of autumn and rose-gold skies of evening, both of which are symbols of aging.

When Alfred, Lord Tennyson, wrote of "sunset and evening star," he was writing about death. William Ernest Henly made similar reference when he wrote: "So be my passing. My task accomplished and the long day done." We have learned to defend against death by reflecting upon the beauty of natural night or the onset of the long winter. Yet this venerable image misses the point of renewal in later years. The person who feels like an old bird roosting out his last days is not about to revitalize and "mount up with wings as eagles."

As years come on, people feel the need of some plausible scenario for what is happening to them. The old-tree image has been around so long and is so much a part of our heritage that many accept it with no thought of other possibilities. I must confess that I shared this view until I became aware of the "surge of the sixties." I read the twelfth chapter of Ecclesiastes with complete agreement. Only now do I see the utter pessimism of that gloomy preacher.

Old age is variously regarded in the Old Testament. Some of the characters exemplified vital renewal, while some others toddled off to their graves gloomy and impaired. Some extolled the bright meaning of the years of wisdom and integrity, while other re-echoed the minor chords of fatalistic despair. Only now have I rediscovered the full impact of such triumphant passages as Psalms 103:3-5. "Bless the Lord, O my soul, and forget not all his benefits; Who forgiveth all thine iniquities; who healeth all thy diseases; who redeemeth thy life from destruction; who crowneth thee with loving kindness and tender mercies; who satisfieth thy mouth with good things; so that thy youth is renewed like the eagles."

Sometimes a colleague says to me, "Pessimism and optimism are subjective appraisals. Some people always expect the worst while others always expect the best." There is truth in his remark, but there is also error. If I say to myself, "Tomorrow will be gloomy," and it turns out to be bright, I may be so intent on the gloomy day that I stay indoors and miss a golden day of summer. If I say, "Aging is a biological necessity and nothing can be done about it; I must accept the inevitable loss of powers and endure with patience the Grim Reaper's approach." Then, to my surprise, if my later years turn out to be filled with the possibility of joy and happiness, my old-tree image of aging may deprive me of the vibrant renewal and achievement which could be mine.

Suppose Goethe had laid down his pen at sixty-five or Churchill had retired to the country at the same age. Our lives would have been deprived of Faust and of freedom.

To look on the final days of life as the onset of winter or the end of the biological life cycle has comfort as well as a measure of reality. The fact that everybody grows old and dies enables me to feel less put upon by fate. Resignation itself is a comfort to some. A vision of renewal, however, is infinitely better. Quite apart from the happiness of the individual, a vision of renewal makes pertinent the boundless possibilities of the vast human resource for human betterment which resides in the growing millions of older people. We are legion, and our talents are sorely needed in a confused and troubled world.

THE EAGLE-WING THEORY

The surge of the sixties has truly given me a second wind for achievement and happiness. Many of my contemporaries are enjoying this same experience and have testified to this effect. With my new insight I have found unmistakable evidence in history, philosophy and biography.

St. Paul testified that renewal comes to the inward man even though the outward man grows old and decrepit. I have found that the eagle-wing theory, declared by the prophet Isaiah, is literally fulfilled in my life. My testimony is joined by a multitude of vibrant old people whose lives are filled with joy and whose talents are a major national and international resource for human betterment.

The eagle has been a symbol of power and endurance for as long as history has been recorded. Classical Greece associated the eagle with Zeus, great father of the gods. The Roman eagle was the symbol of the Empire, and it struck terror in the hearts of Rome's enemies. When the founding fathers of America sought a symbol for the new land, they chose the eagle.

In Bible times the eagle represented speed, longevity, power and indefatigable ability to rise above difficulty. Many varieties of eagles are at home in the lands of the Bible. I have been fascinated morning after morning as I've watched the eagles wheel and glide above Jerusalem, Bethlehem, Nazareth and Jericho. Naturalists report that some live to be more than fifty years old without diminution of power in flight. No better symbol could be found to suggest renewal in later years. Weather and contrary winds only challenge the eagle to more daring and lordly flight. If the lion is the king of beasts, the eagle is surely king of the birds.

Only after my new insight into the age of wisdom and integrity did I catch the full meaning of that great Isaiah passage of scripture. My new burst of energy and my new outlook on life are perfectly described by the regeneration that enables me to "mount up with wings as eagles." I now realize that ancient philosophy also had similar insights into the way in which some older people are renewed. Heraclitus, for example, saw all reality as fire which was forever changing and renewing itself. The human soul separates from eternal fire and continues to renew itself again and again until at death it returns to the universal energy which he called fire. Countervailing forces within reality resulted in development and achievement. This petulant old Ephesian of the sixth century B.C. can be read in various ways, but I see in him the very dim suggestion of a continuing renewal theory of aging.

Although Greek culture was enchanted, almost obsessed with youth, the best of the literary Greeks were patient with age. Plato, for example, wrote of old age with respect and affection which amounted almost to veneration. His most celebrated dialogue, *The Republic*, begins in the home of Cephalon, a ninety-year-old merchant prince, who was clear of mind and quick of wit. Socrates soon found his own brilliant powers of reason challenged by this aged host who loved life and lived it to the full. Socrates, seeing an opportunity to learn something about aging, pressed Cephalon to describe his feelings about money, station, world affairs, health and sex. The old man was so clever and convincing that Socrates hurriedly moved on to the more basic issues of politics and economics which constitute the body of *The Republic.*

In Plato's literary masterpiece, *The Symposium,* the best ideas come not from young Alcibiades or even the young Agathon, but rather from the aging Socrates who claimed to have derived his ideas of love from a very old woman named Diotima. This wise old woman saw the power of love transcending age. Love, she argued, may begin with love of things and progress to love of people. The person who has wisdom may rise to intellectual love, which expresses itself in such forms as reason, beauty, thought and goodness. The truly wise person, however, can transcend all experienced things and deal with love as pure idea above and beyond history.

Plato's high regard for aging is apparent throughout his most celebrated dialogues. In fact Plato proved his respect for age by abandoning his life of ease to study with the aging scholar-teacher Socrates. As a result of studies with the great gadfly of Athens, his own later years were renewed with energy and rich with achievement. Plato freed philosophy from its materialism, mechanism and determinism. In this respect, he prepared the Greek mind for the message of St. Paul who found "faith, hope and love" a more excellent trilogy than "the good, the true and the beautiful." The spiritual had become triumphant.

Henri Bergson is the modern exponent of "vitalism." This brilliant Frenchman, born in 1859, said, "For a conscious being, to exist is to change, to change is to mature, to mature is to go on creating one's self endlessly." Here is a modern Heraclitus who provides a philosophic image of aging as progressive renewal. He locates the fallacy of materialism in our preoccupation with space. Life, however, according to Bergson, is time. Life is duration, and we accumulate experience as we go along. Even when our memory falters, our wills and feelings remember. The aging person has a greater reservoir of experience from which to draw when new challenges require new procedures. Bergson is the pioneer of modern gerontology in its efforts to overcome old age and death. His almost poetic declaration of faith in man's biological future is something to ponder.

The animal takes its stand on the planet, man bestrides animality, and the whole of humanity, in space and time, is one immense army galloping beside and before and behind each of us in an overwhelming charge able to beat down every resistance and clear the most formidable obstacles, perhaps even death.[3]

Many contemporary biologists, physiologists and physicians have confirmed the eagle-wing theory which I have derived from personal experience and from the testimony of many others who have had similar experience. They, like me, have witnessed renewal in older people. I am fully aware of the doctors and scientists who are much more disposed toward the old-car theory or the old-tree theory as

---

3 Bergson, Henri, *Creative Evolution* (New York: Henry Hold and Company, 1911), p. 271.

images of aging. This in no way disturbs me. They are free to view the future in terms of their beliefs and opinions. But I have absolute confidence in the eagle-wing theory. I can only say, "Once I felt old; now I feel renewed!"

Nothing in the universe is more wonderful than a human life. The masterpiece of God's creation was a human being and it still is! A living, breathing, feeling, thinking human being, who can fathom the stars and create beauty, is more awe-inspiring to me than Kant's "starry heavens above and moral universe within." To think of my friends as obsolescent machines or disintegrating vegetation is not only mistaken but, to me, distasteful. Every human being is a child of God and His beautiful creation. Humans can prove themselves unworthy of their parentage, dangerous to society and miserable to themselves; but they are still more than machines and trees.

The human organism can sustain noble persons like Albert Schweitzer and Maude Adams. Who could see the aging Arthur Fiedler on the podium without thinking of renewal in later years? The aging Polycarp at eighty-six, faced with martyrdom, testified to his faith in Jesus Christ and went to his death soaring above his accuser like a mighty eagle. This faith and power is available to anyone who is willing and able to receive it.

The rest of my life appears to me as something very different and exciting since I have found the fountains of renewal for the later years. No more do I carry around a vision of my body as an old car breaking down. Neither do I see myself as an old tree losing its leaves in the autumn as an omen of the fast approaching time when the leaves will come no more in spring and the sturdy old trunk will become a rotting log returning to the earth from which it sprang.

I now look on my life as a series of renewals which come to me periodically as I provide the conditions and "wait upon the Lord." I am vital and strong from the surge of the sixties, and I confidently expect a new burst of energy and achievement in the seventies and in the eighties. I look around me at my contemporaries and thrill at the sight of one who knows renewal. This person is not trying to stay young nor yet is he waiting gloomily for the undertaker. Renewed people accept life as it is with all the verve and élan that God can supply. They cultivate life to the full and learn to enjoy the harvest of every day and every year.

PROVIDING
THE CONDITIONS

The eagle-wing image of aging is no quick release from individual responsibility. Those who "wait upon the Lord" hoping to "mount up with wings as eagles" may wait a long time and face bitter disappointment unless they provide the conditions. Renewal is active rather than passive. The good Lord feeds the birds of the air, but he does not throw the seeds into the nest. He transforms a dry bulb in the mud into a beautiful lily, but he does not do the planting, feeding and cultivating. Renewal, beautiful as it is, is a condition involving responsibility.

My academic colleagues chide me for using a vague term such as "wait upon the Lord." The term seems very precise and clear to me. A physician cannot heal a broken bone or replace damaged tissue. He can, however, provide the conditions for the healing and then he must wait upon the Lord. A farmer cannot cause a blade of wheat or a stalk of corn to grow. He can only prepare the soil, plant the seed, keep down the weeds, water the ground if necessary; then he must wait upon the Lord. Renewal from the bruises and bumps of childhood is not the child's own doing. Recovery from the illnesses and accidents of youth is above and beyond our control. Health and energy which sustain us for the middle years are more providence than self-help. We can nurture and encourage, but life is a gift of God.

My surge of the sixties is no personal achievement. I simply felt the challenge of important things to do and responded. I provided some of the conditions such as caring for my health and relating to stimulating friends, but God did all the rest. His renewal of strength and energy came upon me all at once, as did that St. Louis sunrise. I waited on the Lord. He renewed my strength and I am able to "mount up with wings as eagles."

When I lecture to my colleagues and tell them about my renewal, the universal question is, "How does one find the surge of the sixties?" or "How can I find this Fountain of Age you talk about?" This is a very searching question. My contemporaries divide themselves naturally into those who are renewed and those who are not. I have some charming friends who have resigned themselves to withdraw and progressively disintegrate. They beautifully illustrate the traditional images of aging as a sad thing that everybody must go through. That beautiful little poet Phyllis McGinley wrote at seventy:

"Seventy is bitterness
Seventy is gall
But it is better to be seventy
Than not alive at all."

I have other friends, thank God, and they are many, who share my sense of renewal. They face the world with verve and hope. They have looked old age full in the face and found it beautiful. I can say with absolute fidelity that I am happier now than I have ever been in my life. Growing numbers of older people feel this way.

The really big question is how to change from grim resignation to hope and expectation. There are several things that can be done, the first of which is the affirmation of individual responsibility. Each person is a general manager of his own life. Each person is free to dwindle down toward oblivion or to undertake the thrilling adventure of renewal. I think of ten definite guidelines that have been helpful to me. I have formulated them into the ten commandments for those who would find renewal.

1. You must find a new vision of what the rest of your life can be.
2. You must take charge of your own life.
3. You must give attention to your health.
4. You must find a challenging project.
5. You must have definite things to do.
6. You must cultivate new friendships.
7. You must find new interests.
8. You must find new ways to play and recover some old ones.
9. You must take time to think about problems and possibilities.
10. You must affirm life. There is untold power in a positive attitude.

GETTING A NEW VISION

Today is the first day of the rest of your life! Look ahead and what do you see? If you see nothing but hardening arteries, loss of hearing, loss of vision, inactivity, withdrawal from work and play, loneliness and steady decline toward the grave, you can throw this book away right now. Renewal comes to those who have the expectant heart. If, as you look ahead, you see a wide variety of things to do, places to go, possibilities to realize, with a gift of power to meet each new challenge, then you have provided the prime condition for renewal.

Sculptors in Florence passed by a giant block of granite time after time without enough vision to see what could be done with it. Michelangelo came along. He looked at it as he passed each day trying to get an image of something beautiful within that solid block. At long last his vision came. He went to work with his hammer and chisel and created that handsome statue of David which now stands in the Tribune of the Gallery of the Academia in Florence. David, without the artist, would still be imprisoned in that solid block of stone. Men and women looked at the stars for centuries oblivious to the interrelationship of all the heavenly bodies until Isaac Newton, an apple having bounced off his scientific head, formulated his laws of motion. The beauty of the cedar waxwings in spring, or the finch with his sunshine coat to replace his green of winter, may pass unnoticed to the eye which lacks interest and ardor. The varied leaves which come down as an avalanche of color in the autumn may be nothing but a troublesome nuisance to the undiscerning eye.

Lift up your eyes to tomorrow, next year and the rolling centuries ahead. Become aware of the promises and joys that await you. Face the challenges with courage, and all at once you will find your life renewed. One day at a time is an important requirement for living, but one day ahead is not enough. A renewed person has an ardent and expectant eye for all future days.

I know from firsthand experience what a new image of aging can mean. I have tried living with a stubborn effort to stay young in accordance with the old-car theory, and I have tried living with the acceptance and courage of the old-tree theory. Now that I see the rest of my life from the lofty vision of the soaring eagle, I have truly discovered the fountain of age which the good Lord promised through Isaiah the Prophet. Boundless resources await the person who has the ardent eye and the expectant heart.

TAKE CHARGE OF YOUR OWN LIFE

David Riesman in his *Lonely Crowd* saw our generation as "other directed." We tend to do what is expected of us. The opinions of our families and friends lay down the parameters for our lives. Individual freedom and initiative are difficult to achieve and are downright frightening to many people. However, the person who has given control of his life over to other people has missed the opportunity for renewal in later years. Now is the time to take charge of your own life. The promises of "mount up with wings as eagles" are only for those who are willing to try their own wings.

The person who can do nothing but what is expected of him does not find it easy to take charge of his life. He is already comfortable in his rigid conformity. The stakes are high, however. Those who are content to follow the American generalization of "growing old gracefully" face resignation, a little bit of travel, some busy-work, withdrawal from life, and a fairly early death. Those who have the courage and initiative to live their own lives take charge and thereby provide one important condition for renewal. Playing out the role of public expectations provides no occasion and no challenge that will elicit a new surge of power and achievement.

The person who would be renewed must "wait upon the Lord" as a free and individual person willing to run the risk of managing his own life. This means he must shake off the chains of conformity that enslave him. Vocational experience has a tendency to control the life of any person who reaches the exciting age of the sixties and the ensuing years. If a person's work is of such a nature that he is forced to retire against his will, he may rail against fate, the company, the rules and the law, but to no avail. If he cannot keep working at his old job, let him find a new one.

Some of the happiest vocational moments of any life come with a new commitment in the middle sixties or thereafter. My good friend Oscar Dunn was executive vice president of General Electric. He could have retired in comfort and even opulence, but instead he has chosen to take on the enormous challenge and responsibility of serving as chief executive for the Chamber of Commerce for New York City.

The "fun city" is notorious for its fiscal problems. Crime gets out of hand from time to time. The slums and ghettos are disorganized and depressing. Oppressive taxation along with other problems has caused many businesses and industries to leave the city. Yet Oscar Dunn has taken up the challenge of bringing a new vision of promise and a new image of hope. Able people such as Walter Wriston of Citicorp, William Ellinghaus of American Telephone and Telegraph Company, and several of their colleagues in finance, business and industry have joined in an effort for renewal in that great city.

Under the new leadership, the Chamber of Commerce raised money from the private sector to restore the businesses destroyed by looting in a recent electrical blackout. The leaders in New York have a new attitude. Men of business and finance have encouraged the politicians and civil servants to take on the disciplines necessary for the fabulous but difficult urban area. I see Oscar Dunn from time to time. Instead of being over-burdened with these crushing responsibilities, he is a man of renewed energy, power, ability and achievement. In taking charge of his own life, he literally exemplifies the vision of Isaiah who said, "They shall mount up with wings as eagles." A second career of this kind is available to most everyone who can marshall the resourcefulness, patience, initiative and perseverance required. Not everyone will be able to do anything as dramatic as a New York City renascence, but he may have a more satisfying life.

Some people miss the opportunity for taking charge of their own lives because of the influence and expectations of their families. Many tend to internalize family habits. A mother who has always worked for her children may go right on working for them even though the children are long grown and much better able to manage their own lives than she is. A father may turn over his funds to his children and thereby become dependent upon them.

For reasons of their own, families often discourage the remarriage of a surviving parent without regard to the importance of companionship in the golden years. Families on occasion encourage aging parents to enter rest homes prematurely or to settle for useless and dependent roles unsuited for those who are able to do many things on their own initiative. Each older person who learns to "wait upon the Lord" must have a declaration of independence and be able to say, "God has given me the rest of my life, and it is my responsibility to manage it to the best of my ability."

Communities also have a way of controlling the lives of people through subtle public opinion. If a person lives in a town where old people are expected to live and act in a certain way, the oldster must have real courage to strike out on his own. A gentleman who dresses well and enjoys feminine companionship may become the object of ridicule and jibes such as "No fool like an old fool!" Marriage is usually the happiest career for mature widows, but the one who makes herself attractive to the few available men is likely to hear catty remarks from her neighbors. Those who have the courage to live their own lives must pay some penalties. Our society appears to feel a mild and indulgent contempt for old people. This makes the challenge all the greater for all who would take charge of their own lives.

From childhood on, peer groups dominate our lives. The patterns established in a tight community have so much bearing on the way aging people conduct their lives that certain communities are notable for longevity and others for the fact that their senior citizens die young. One little town in England, for example, has many centenarians, while a nearby village has few that live past eighty. The people of Abkhazia in the Russian Caucasus are notorious for their longevity. So many of them live beyond one hundred years that it has become commonplace and expected. The tradition of physical exercise, both at work and at play, together with abstemious living and limited diet in the context of an abiding family relationship, reduces stress and brings peace of mind. The environment and the customs provide the basis for long life and, in addition, for joy, achievement and zest for living in advanced years.

In such beneficially structured communities, conformity is not much of a problem. American society, however, imposes expectations on aging citizens which shorten life and take much of the joy out of what little time there is in the later years. For these reasons, it is even more essential for the people who would find fulfillment in the time of integrity and wisdom to affirm responsibility for their own lives. Conditions for renewal in America include creative management of one's own affairs in later years. Living one's own life is an important condition for those who would "wait upon the Lord" in such a way that His gift of renewal can be received. Those who slavishly follow the expectations of the community might as well die young because there is very little fun in moving to a rest home and complaining about life in general.

The greatest enemy of self-management in later years is habit. When Charles Dickens wrote his

Tale of Two Cities, he pictured an old doctor incarcerated in the Bastille, where his days and nights alike were dark and his only consolation was working with a last and hammer repairing shoes. After years of this busy-work, the revolutionary mob battered down the doors of the prison. Members of the old doctor's family took him to the pleasant freedom of the British countryside where there were birds flying through sunny skies against fluffy clouds and leafy horizons. The old doctor, however, began to complain and ask for his hammer, his last and his shoes. He was finally comfortable only when he was put in a dark closet and given his shoemaker's equipment. He could not bear the sunlight and the freedom. Habit had captured him and put him in chains. Almost anybody with a little encouragement can break the chains of habit and find joy and zest in life. The essential first step is the desire and determination to take charge of one's life in the final years.

ATTEND TO YOUR HEALTH

The all-powerful and all-loving God of Isaiah could not renew the prophet's strength as promised unless Isaiah provided the conditions. Then and now taking care of one's health is a prime condition. Robbing people of renewal are conditions such as gluttony, chain smoking, pickling one's vitals in alcohol, living on dope even though it may be medically prescribed, constant stress, lack of exercise, lack of rest and sleep. Those who would "wait upon the Lord" start out by giving careful consideration to the habits, disciplines and requirements of a sound mind in a sound body.

Everybody works out his own system of staying alive. The will to live accounts for human existence on this planet. Misguided appetite, however, or preoccupation with some peripheral concern can override that natural human inclination to survive. How many times I have seen victims of emphysema smoke themselves to death or alcoholics commit slow suicide. How many of my friends eat themselves to obesity as they march blindly toward an early grave. Formulae for health are complicated and subject to individual taste, inclination, custom and conditions. The person who would find golden joy in later years must become a wise and efficient manager of his own health. God helps those who help themselves.

FIND A CHALLENGING PROJECT

I have talked with some of the most expert and perceptive people in America and Great Britain about the surge of the sixties. Those who have experienced renewal in later years nearly always mention something challenging to do as a major factor. My study of biography definitely confirms the importance of the stimulus that comes from a demanding project. My colleague John Taylor points to the productive later years of many musicians. He mentions offhand such notables as Toscanini, Koussevitsky, Casals, Rubenstein and Stokowski. The challenge that comes from writing, conducting or performing music is almost boundless and is a major factor in the creative later years of great musicians.

Arnold Toynbee saw response to challenge as the principal factor in the survival of an individual. In my own life, I see the challenge that came from assuming responsibility on several boards of business corporations as a significant factor in the surge of the sixties. In my long career as a teacher and college president, my business talents were somewhat subordinated. As director of a large industrial corporation, however, I am able to fulfill portions of my unlived life and utilize some hitherto undeveloped talents that would otherwise be lost forever. My academic colleagues who have retired to some exciting new posts not only live longer but are more fun.

One of the happiest and most successful examples of a new challenge came to my late friend Harry Houghton, who had spent his career as a shipping clerk for Ford Motor Company. When mandatory retirement caught up with him he became the financial secretary and treasurer of a large metropolitan church. In this capacity, he took on new life. His blood pressure became normal and his cheeks rosy as his daily responsibilities found a natural rhythm and his unused talents became apparent. He could hardly wait for the next day to go to work. He was cheerful, friendly, thoughtful, delightful and attentive to his work right up until the time when old age called a halt. Look around you and you will see that the people who take on a challenging project put themselves in line for renewal.

GET SOME DEFINITE THINGS TO DO

Death stalks the person who is always wondering what to do. The person who moves from one meaningful responsibility to another, however, finds strength for the day and renewal for the years ahead. An overworked and harassed employee may long for a time when there is nothing to do, but such a time, when it arrives, is lethal. Retired executives are astonished that they miss the phone calls and interruptions that once bugged them. They miss going to the office. They miss the people who came to them for advice. They miss the sense of importance that comes from the office, from routine responsibilities and other similar demands. The tyranny of the clock as it brings deadlines to the overworked and overworried person seems unbearable, but the person who has no deadlines is a candidate for the morgue. Nothing forbids renewal more effectively than absence of definite things to do. Resourceful people always find things that require attention and even demand a certain amount of routine. Astute people arrange for continuing responsibility.

Any person who would set the stage for a period of renewal does well to find a pattern for life that combines daily responsibilities and demands with freedom for new and different things. Not everyone can stay on a familiar assignment as do some judges who elect not to retire, or a physician who goes on practicing for many years. Not everyone can take a new job or enter some new profession such as might be involved in starting a new business. Not everyone can take up some new creative work such as writing, painting, composing, craft work or any of the creative or performing arts. Not everyone can find contentment in the responsibilities of home and community. Not everyone can become engrossed in voluntary service to church or local service centers such as hospitals and character-building agencies. Everybody, however, can find a life pattern that affords some definite things to be done, and can relate to these things in such a way that there are no problems of panic, the panic that comes from not knowing what to do next or the discouragement that comes from feeling useless.

The fact that many women elect to be home-makers may be an important factor in their longevity. Nobody retires from a home. There are always definite things to do around a house, many of them requiring considerable resourcefulness and initiative. Many women become quite involved in their communities and develop a set of responsibilities and an impressive array of challenges. From these things there is no retirement. Many men and some professional women, however, depend on an occupation for a sense of worth and standing in the community. Without their jobs, they feel they have lost their standing. The very fact that their jobs commanded a salary added to their sense of self-esteem.

On balance, however, women seem to find more fulfillment in activities other than a specific job in an office, a factory, a field or in any other sort of vocational past. For this reason, I believe, women tend to be less frustrated with retirement and somewhat less inclined to be problems to themselves and to other people. They have things to do and promises to keep which prolong their years and brighten their lives.

CULTIVATE NEW FRIENDSHIPS

Eagerness to develop new friendships is an index of vitality in any person at any age, but it becomes very important in later years. Some of the friends of childhood and youth have changed, and pursuit of other interests has weakened the ties. Some are no longer living. New occasions bring new friends with new interests and characteristics that inspire new activities and afford new satisfaction. In my own case, new friendships have done as much as anything else in my life to bring about renewal and excitement for maturity. The people around me who have experienced the surge of the sixties are people who meet new people, develop new friendships and explore new interests.

Friendship cannot be forced. We can only provide the conditions and allow the friendship to grow. I marvel at the way in which my students develop their friendships by virtue of the positions they occupy in the classroom. When I was teaching large classes at the beginning of my career, the students were seated alphabetically. I noticed that those whose names began with "A" became friends with those whose names began with "A" or "B", while those with "Z" or "W" were more than likely to develop friendships with each other. One of the principal factors that promotes love among animals is physical juxtaposition. My zookeeper friends tell me of a male and female tiger who despised each other until they were placed in adjoining cages. After a few weeks, the cage door was opened and they came together and mated and lived happily ever after.

Mutual appreciation is a great factor in providing the conditions for friendship to grow. Self-centered people seldom have many friends. As people grow older, they have more insight and understanding as well as time to practice friendship. Lasting delight can come from a golfing acquaintance or delightful companionship around the bridge table. People who work together in some selfless cause become involved with one another. Those who face danger together are ever intertwined. Common interest and common ideas make for a pleasant relationship but some of the most enduring and remarkable friendships have been among people who disagree violently in such things as philosophy, politics and life styles. Acceptance and understanding are absolutely essential. I have watched friendship develop throughout my three score years and ten and have come to the conclusion that older people are more capable of deep and abiding friendship than are the young. New friends in the sixties, seventies and eighties can open up new horizons, new areas of interest and exciting projects that help one find the renewal essential to vibrant later life.

NEW INTERESTS

A new interest can transform an aging person into an eager and vital candidate for renewal. Some of the most remarkable people I know have come alive because of interests developed after three score years. A prime example is Willard Merrihue, who retired as a highly-placed executive at General Electric and moved to Naples, Florida. Instead of joining with those who work themselves to death attempting to play, he became president of the Audubon Society. In turn, this, with his unusual talents and the natural leadership which inspired people to work with him, brought him into a pleasant relationship with the newly formed Collier County Conservancy. He has exercised an enormous influence in Florida and a considerable influence in the entire country. Generous people have given money and land to preserve the wilderness. Denizens of the Everglades seem to express their gratitude by the very delight with which they go about living their lives in those warm and tranquil waters and mangrove islands. Instead of being an old man at seventy-five, Willard Merrihue is vibrant and renewed.

My neighbor, Kurt Fox comes to mind. He is a retired executive of the Young Men's Christian Association. New interests took precedence over his inclination to sit, remember and enjoy. He began organizing travel parties to the four corners of the earth. A Kurt Fox pilgrimage is more than just a tour. He knows how to promote friendship and bring excitement to the travelers. Strange lands become more significant and more beautiful because of this renewed person.

Sometimes a long and successful career can have an exciting afterglow which amounts to a whole new interest. Dr. W. A. Hudson of Detroit, who came to be president of the World College of Chest Physicians, retired from an illustrious career as a thoracic surgeon. He went back to his home farm in the mountains of Arkansas. Farming had once been his interest, and his ability to grow things was not only undiminished but enhanced. His real condition for renewal came, however, when he began to practice a limited amount of general medicine for the benefit of his Arkansas neighbors. The mountain folk love him. In their minds, he is not the world-renowned surgeon whose name appears in *Who's Who in the World*, but their neighbor who studied medicine and knows how to help them when they are sick. His years are many, but he has truly found the fountain of age and his strength is renewed.

It is only natural that an aging person has his own interests. It would be dreadful if everyone wished to do the same thing. If a person has a unique talent, it may be developed in later years when retirement relieves him of the demanding vocational responsibilities. My good friend, Edward Spencer was chief finance officer for Detroit Edison. In this capacity, he dealt with some of the most highly skilled accountants, investors, security analysts, managers and executives in the world. Upon retirement he moved to Georgia where he soon became interested in higher education. Then, his interest became so great that he said farewell to Georgia and retired to the rigors of Detroit to teach at his alma mater, Lawrence Institute of Technology. His influence on the young is salutory. His vast experience is utilized and his new interest has made him a prime candidate for renewal. In biblical language, he has learned to wait upon the Lord and his strength is renewed.

PLAY

Alfred North Whitehead, famed British mathematician and philosopher, wrote a small book called *Aims of Education.* The punch line of the book was his remark that the chief aim of all education is joy. Joy is an essential prerequisite to renewal in later years. Only the happy people find the fountain of age. Play is a considerable factor in the joyful life. Too many busy people have neglected the art of play in the hassle of middle years. At a time of added leisure, the art may be difficult to recover. Play requires some deliberate planning and attention at any time in life. The older person, however, may have the necessary time and inclination to practice and improve. I marvel at the skill involved in some shuffleboard matches played by the residents of retirement homes and villages. Some golfers do not really find their game until they are well past the time of retirement when they have more time to play. Bridge is at its best with the mature.

Play is mental and emotional as well as physical. The sophisticated humor of musicians, poets, lecturers and even mathematicians is rare delight. Some of the world's greatest humorists have been past seventy before their talent came into full flower. Benjamin Franklin had more fun when his sixties were a memory. Bob Hope is far more effective now than he was at thirty or even sixty! Crossword puzzles are a form of intellectual play. Humor on television enjoys an enviable rating. The vicarious delight that comes to those who attend theater and sporting events affords release from inner tension and provides a spectator's sense of participation. The value is far greater if the person is actually a part of the fun, but vicarious sport and theater are not to be downplayed. They have a part in supplying the need for play and thereby help to provide part of the conditions necessary for renewal. The emotional value of such activities is to be found in the release which Aristotle called catharsis.

The older person in search of the fountain of age, however, does well to get at a more direct kind of play. Whether it be tennis, golf, swimming, boating, bowling, skating or hiking, he does well to study the sport to improve his play. The thrill of any sport is enhanced by superior performance. The older player need not win in competition, although there is no reason why he should not if he has what it takes; but the important thing for the renewal preparation is a sense of doing well by one's own standards. A severly handicapped person who walks around the block may have enjoyed as much of a sense of victory as does the Olympic athlete who wins the decathlon. The older person beginning on skis may find real satisfaction in a short hill that would seem boring to an experienced skier.

Social play does still more for the player when it is done well. Dancers have more fun when they can improve the rather difficult art of adapting one's feet to the various rhythms. Entertaining is great fun when it is done skillfully. Cooking can be an exciting form for men as well as for women. The art of social conversation is a rewarding form of play, and the person who does it well finds friends as well as satisfaction in it.

Older people find challenge and renewal in vital participation in various forms of play. An eighty-four year old man is a champion swimmer in the Pacific Northwest. Many older golfers are able to shoot their age. One of my cronies, Charles Lawson, at eighty-four does just that and takes pride in having played with the same ball for four years! Much first-rate tennis is played by those over sixty-five! An octogenarian friend of mine is very proud of having won the cross-country ski trophy against a tough field in Sun Valley on a recent occasion.

Since my dramatic renewal in the sixties I have begun to sing again. I was a basso profundo in my college days. I sang with the varsity quartet and did some solos at the glee club concerts. Then for almost fifty years I did not sing at all. On my seventieth birthday I startled my colleagues by singing one of the old songs from my college days. Since then, I have been rehearsing some contem-

porary songs that fit my low voice. I have entertained the chapter of the American Association of
Retired Persons with a couple of Broadway hit
tunes. The play value to me is very substantial. I
feel genuinely renewed, and my friends are amazed
as well as entertained.

THOUGHT AND REFLECTION

There is an unmistakable rhythm in life. The
archer hits the target partly by drawing the bow
and partly by letting go. The crew sends a racing
shell flying over the water to the coxswain's
rhythmic count. Life is best described by a principle of alternation between effort and relaxation.
The clever author of *Inner Tennis* reduced the complex process to "bounce, hit." Whether in work or
play the candidate for renewal will need to find a
way to let go and think about things after he has
worked for maximum achievement. Call it meditation if you wish; I call it prayer and reflection. I find
the practice of the presence of God to be a joyful
and significant discipline for my thoughts. Each
person must find his own method of thinking about
things and getting it all together.

Doctor Borge in Ingmar Bergman's *Wild Strawberries* found this clue to integrity in the interpreta-
tion of his dreams. He was a practicing psychiatrist
and could read his own past in his dreaming. Every
person who seeks renewal in later life must find
some way to bring his whole lifetime together. This
search for what Erik Erikson calls "integrity" is an
essential and beneficial characteristic need of older
persons. Everyone does something of this kind by
recalling and relating long-ago incidents in his
lifetime. Only the attentive, however, do it well

enough to aid and encourage the renewal which enables him to "mount up with wings as eagles." The deliberate search for integrity is an important condition for changing life from a dirge to a dance.

AFFIRM LIFE

Ponce de Leon did not find the Fountain of Youth. Nobody has found the Fountain of Youth because nobody can become young again, and nobody stays young. People can hide their age to appear young, or pretend by word and behavior to be younger, but Father Time is not easily deceived. The Fountain of Age, however, is a different matter. I have experienced the Fountain of Age in my own life and I have observed its beautiful influence in the lives of others; Helen Hayes, for example, in a recent interview said: "Somehow I expected seventy-seven to be a decrepit, enfeebled age that happened only to other people. But this age isn't that way at all. Inside I still feel just like a kid." (*Modern Maturity,* April-May, 1978, p. 14.)

I can honestly and carefully say that I feel more happy and alive in my seventies than I did at forty, fifty or sixty. Even the twenties and thirties come back to me as full of aspirations and concerns that kept me from full enjoyment. I was more interested in what I could be than in what I was. My obsessions have fallen away with time and renewal. The Fountain of Age has brought me joy and happiness, and these are the stuff of life!

Only those who have what Edna Millay calls the ardent eye recognize the Fountain of Age when they come upon it. The surge of the sixties is for those who expect it, recognize it and enjoy it. The others stumble past on the way to the grave, missing all the fun and zest that come with renewal. Challenging things to do, affirmation of the joy of life, sensitivity to the needs of others, discovery, new ideas and new enterprises—these make the difference between a radiant life in later years and the dull march toward the terminus.

I have wrapped up the whole idea of providing conditions for renewal in one imperative: "AFFIRM LIFE." Many people fail to do it. They are so accustomed to thinking in conventional terms of death as the natural goal of life that they miss the triumphant opportunities of the best years of their lives. The person who can say "yes" to life, however, will "mount up with wings as eagles." Death will come, but only as an episode in a victorious and exciting life which feels the crescendo effect of the Fountain of Age.

RETIREMENT AND RENEWAL

Periods of renewal in later life are closely related to vocation and, therefore, to retirement. The very idea of retirement is satisfaction for some and tragedy for others. Whether you retire from the particular position which has become an important part of your career is a matter to be worked out between yourself and the company. For those who are self-employed, the situation can be more easily resolved by a careful judgment based on clients, customers, patients and others involved. To retire or not is an individual matter.

In cases of mandatory retirement there may be some problems. Elsewhere in this book I have referred to that great American musician, composer, conductor and producer, Don Gillis, whose forced retirement may well have cost his life. Mandatory retirement can be a traumatic experience for many people, but this problem can be handled with resourcefulness, counseling and preparation.

Those who do not need to retire and who do not wish to may very well be among those best fitted for renewal if they have the vision and provide the necessary conditions. Among my friends who best exemplify this kind of renewal is Leonard Read, founder and president of the Foundation for Economic Education, Irvington-on-Hudson, New York. Dr. Read has celebrated his eightieth birthday and is as able in his administration, writing, lecturing, and teaching as he has been at any time in his long career. At seventy he wrote a book called *The Coming Aristocracy*. The three paragraphs which begin Chapter Two, "In Quest of Maturity," describe very well his perception of his own periods of renewal:

> This is my favorite book, not because it is better than the other books, but because it is later. Every one of its nineteen chapters has been written in an eight-month period surrounding my seventieth birthday and with no let-up in travel, lectures, or other chores. These chapters represent attempts at attaining some measure of maturity against the stubborn opposition which the senior years tend to impose. It is my contention that longevity is for the sake of maturity, not longevity.
>
> Does life really begin at forty, as popular expression has it? Or does it begin, instead, with each moment one grows in awareness, perception, consciousness? Is not the budding process a continuous beginning? The moons that have come and gone do not necessarily measure growth or its ending; now and then life flags in the teens; on occasion it accelerates in the nineties. If seventy seems less likely than forty for a new beginning, the reason is that so many have died on the vine in that interval.
>
> Glory to the man who can truthfully attest, "Life begins at ninety!"[1]

---

1 Read, Leonard E., *The Coming Aristocracy* (New York: Foundation for Economic Education, 1969), p. 7.

An ideal situation, in my opinion, would be an arrangement through which an employee and employer would be free to work out a retirement time which is mutually acceptable. This would give the flexibility which the individual needs and which the company, in turn, must have. But for many reasons this arrangement runs into procedural difficulties. Broad policies that apply equally to all involved are much easier to administer than are individual retirement arrangements.

In the end it is the responsibility of the individuals involved to find the new vocational opportunities essential for the periods of renewal which can come in later years. My personal experience is pertinent. I have found my retirement to be most pleasant but only because I have a whole new set of deadlines and responsibilities. I sit on five corporate boards, serve as a consultant and continue to work with the college to which I devoted one-half of my professional career. I continue to do some teaching, which is at the very heart of my lifelong vocational commitment. My feelings about retirement, which I put down on paper shortly after age sixty-five when the event took place, were these:

THE JOYS OF RETIREMENT

I retired at sixty-five after 20 years as president of Bethany College. This plan was announced a full year in advance to provide lead time for the selection of a new president. I soon discovered that some people take a dim view of retirement, while others can hardly wait for it to come. Congratulations and condolences came pouring in from my friends. Those against retirement began asking me, "What will you do now?" This confirmed my impression that fear and dread of retirement springs from the absence of ways and means to utilize one's time and talent. Those who look forward to retirement are those who are eager to get at something they have in mind to do. After two decades of total devotion to Bethany College, I had developed a backlog of long-planned but neglected things to do. When asked how I viewed my retirement, I answered, "With mixed emotions—mixed between joy and ecstasy!"

Serving for twenty years as president of a college was somewhat comparable to having twenty children: I loved every one of them, but I would have done anything in my power to avoid having another one. Not only was my life completely consumed with administrative concerns and responsibilities, but my wife, Aleece, who came to Bethany as a bride, found her life totally consumed by the interests of this honorable old institution. We gave everything we had—time, imagination, care, hope, dreams, hard work and money—to the education of young people. We were on call twenty-four hours a day every day in every year. Even when we traveled abroad, our every concern and interest centered in our service to higher learning. Our social lives were built around promotion of the college. We entertained, visited, addressed, passed the hat, attended conferences, worked with our able staff, scrounged, wheedled and sacrificed for the students and our colleagues in the enterprise. No wonder we could hardly wait for retirement.

Apart from some lingering problems at Bethany College—which disturbed our tranquillity and consumed our time—the transition to our other interests has been very pleasant. We have continued to assist the cause of higher education in every possible way; but we now have time to travel, write and otherwise work and play at our own pace. I have carefully noted the factors involved in adjustment to retirement, and I have concluded that freedom from responsibility is the greatest satisfaction. My commitment was so complete that I felt personally defeated when a project failed or a gift was denied. The concern of every student and teacher had been my concern. Upon retirement, I began to breathe more easily and enjoy life more. This joy is available to everybody who retires with some engaging interests to replace the responsibilities of his previous work-a-day commitment.

But the joy of retirement is not so much absence of responsibility as it is freedom from the demands that consume all time, thought and energy. Nobody wishes to be irresponsible; he wishes to be responsible for some other things that have been neglected. The salesman who has been always out for the order and the person who has been slave to the time clock understand what I mean by the term "freedom." The retired person can take charge of his own life and begin to manage it. The satisfac tion of setting our own priorities and arranging our own schedule is very great. One wise and beautiful wife and mother named Ivabell Harlan, who had reared a large family, found so much satisfaction in her new freedom that she said, "I have just dicovered that I am now eighteen!" She has made good use of her freedom. She is chairman of a large company and president of the Writer's League; and she journeyed to Athens to take first honors in the seminar celebrating the twenty-four hundredth anniversary of Plato.

Retired persons who do not engage in some productive effort tend to die young. Leaving the former job, office, career, does not mean living under the lotus trees. It means freedom to choose the productive work which is available and appealing. Chet Huntley was an able executive at Big Sky, Montana, after his retirement from NBC. Robert Goheen became chairman of The Council on Foundations after retiring as president of Princeton. Dean Rusk is a most effective professor at the University of Georgia after his many years in government. Retired military people wind up in a variety of interesting careers. The very best volunteer service at hospitals, churches and civic clubs is provided by the senior generation who have earned the freedom to do what needs doing.

The retiree who loves life and is willing to live it for a good long while should keep busy. Everybody needs certain definite things to do in order to provide a sense of personal worth and enhance the rhythm of life. It is people who try doing nothing, or who feel they are no longer useful, who die young. A holiday with no responsibility may sound like heaven when the telephone is ringing, five people are waiting in the office, a stack of mail needs answering and unfinished tasks are everywhere; but the experience of having nothing to do is frightening and tends toward depression. The futility of doing nothing that seems important is self-defeating. Dr. Robert N. Butler, Director of the National Institute for Aging, says, "It is important to maintain a continuing investment in activities. That means having specific goals and tasks—belonging to certain clubs, having certain obligations, having a calendar of certain things to do each day. Folks who do this tend to live longer."

The person who retires, moves away and loses contact with his old friends, must find new friends and a new home. Friendships mean more as the years roll by. The wise oldster makes new friends, but cultivates the old ones. I find myself enjoying the people I knew fifty years ago more now than I did when I was in the middle years, hard at work and busy with professional responsibilities and demands. Retired executives find it difficult to write letters. They have had secretarial help all their lives and have forgotten how to spell, if they ever knew. They are embarrassed to search and punch typewriter keys only to produce a sloppy letter. Consideration for other people forbids that they should write longhand. Fortunate indeed are those who find some adequate secretarial assistance for their days of retirement. The telephone, however, is always available at modest expense. Some long distance calls on the budget can bring joy and prolong life.

Another important rule is to live happily with your spouse. Dr. Robert N. Butler said, "Having a partner is very crucial to survival. It may be two people have an emotional involvement that keeps them alive; or it could be the advantage of having someone who can care for you if you're sick." God pity the couples who retire and fight. Family quarrels may be bearable when one or both is working, but when both are at home all the time, sparks fly. The aggressive energy once invested in hard work now comes out in anger, petulance, resentment, harsh words and prickly attitudes. This is the basis for one of my clever friend's remarks concerning her mate's retirement: "Retirement for me means half as much money and twice as much husband."

I enjoy playing golf with my wife more than with anybody else. She is charming company for travel. Shared opinions, as well as shared loves, are pleasant. We know the same people and laugh at the same jokes. We feel free to differ without being full of rancor. We even enjoy each other's eccentricities. Believe me, retirement is more fun if you can enjoy friendly relations with your spouse.

Among the great joys of retirement is the opportunity for self-fulfillment. Now is the time to read books, write the unwritten lines, walk the recondite paths and follow the lure of dim trails. "Unlived life" is a problem to almost everybody. The person who sits and drums on the table is in trouble. He who follows only a rigid pattern and has to do things in a certain precise way has been trapped by meaningless habit and routine. The latter part of life is a crucial period for carrying out those plans that are unfulfilled and have been denied. The rich harvest of wisdom far surpasses the springtime promise of abounding energy.

Another great reward of earned retirement is that one has time to dream. The dreams of advanced age are more frequent, and more significant. They cover the universe and span all time. The limitations of time and space do not apply. In dreams, you can walk a childhood pathway with a friend long gone, stroll leisurely up the Acropolis at Athens, or walk the Royal Mile at Edinburgh. You can dream about Mars and the wheeling systems beyond our solar region. Old loves, old friends, old hopes come back as the golden sun declines.

Perhaps the greatest joy of retirement is the inner peace that comes from the realization that the new freedom is well earned. Self-employed persons delay retirement and sometimes do not retire at all. The crisis which often results in going from working to non-working hits hardest when the retirement is forced and when one feels coerced into leaving a pleasant employment. Our society must face up to the fact that our arbitrary retirement system does not work very well and is wasteful of talent. Nevertheless, the person who can think through the problem until he sees that he has earned the right to live his own life at his own pace finds joy. He may and often does outlive the person who keeps on working until he dies with his boots on. Life is vital and rich for people who can be resourceful enough to hold on to the best in the past and reach out to the best in the future.

The "joys of retirement" which seemed important to me five or six years ago seem insignificant in comparison to the sixties and seventies which I have enjoyed since then. These renewals came about, in part, because I had many challenging things to do, each of which I think called forth the best within me. They came about, in part, also because I was freed from the day-to-day responsibilities. Without the combination of freedom from institutional responsibility and the whole range of new and exciting things to do, I would be toddling off benignly toward the grave as I fully expected to do when I retired.

The "wings as eagles" philosophy of life has been my salvation. I have never been as happy as I am right now. I have found this same attitude true of many people. A perfect illustration is that talented architect Philip Johnson, who said in a Cleveland interview, "When I turned 70, it was like beginning again ... everything gets easier: I don't have to prove anything anymore. I can say to hell with everything."

Whether one retires or not, therefore, is far less important than how that person can provide the conditions conducive to periods of renewal, those periods which can transform the later years into the exciting period of achievement earned by a long life of effective service and performance.

RENEWAL AND PERSISTENT PROBLEMS

Those who drink at the Fountain of Age find a whole new attitude toward life. Problems which seem insurmountable become routine for the renewed person. A little reflection will demonstrate this. Consider, for example, how baffling a problem can seem in the middle of a sleepless night, and how amenable to solution it appears in the light of a bright day after a good breakfast. Consider the "overwhelmed" feeling in facing a difficult problem when health is bad and resistance is low. Then think about how easy the solution appears when vibrant health has returned. This same principle, in still more dramatic fashion, can be applied to the problems of life when they are viewed with a renewed attitude such as the vision of the soaring eagle. The whole world takes on new meaning and excitement when you utilize the outlook of renewal.

This does not mean that all problems vanish. They do not. People will always know anxiety. Many feel worthless and lonely. Some allow themselves to get out of hand and become self-centered. No matter how neatly packaged a person may think himself to be, he is still pretty small when he is merely wrapped up in himself. A careful study of the persistent problems that plague older people shows that the magic of renewal casts new light on all of these problems. When they come in the form of trouble and discouragement, however, we are faced with understanding the universal nature of the difficulties, together with the way in which they develop and the way in which renewal can cope with them.

PERSISTENT PROBLEMS

Experience and reflection indicate that discouragement and depression are among the most difficult—and the most persistent—problems of the latter part of the life cycle. Depression is a problem at any age, of course. Many young people become so depressed that their performance is impaired. When I mention depression as a problem for older people, I am not referring to anything pathological. The slowing processes of the body are reflected in psychological states of mind. Anybody is easily discouraged when he is tired, and weariness is a common complaint of many people.

An illness can trigger a difficult case of "the blues." This vague feeling of unhappiness is often marked by pessimism and a diminution of hope. Emotional persons may seek relief in tears. Those with alcoholic tendencies may try to drink themselves out of the mood. Pill-takers may search for relief with various drugs. Those who simply face their periods of depression tend to tough it out, with a consequent loss of joy and tranquility.

Since depression is closely related to attitudes, as well as to physical conditions, there are ways in which this persistent problem can be relieved. The medical profession is the best source of help at the physical level, although exercise, especially games such as golf, tennis or similar physical diversions, can be very helpful. The problem of attitude is more difficult. Discouragement is best handled when it is faced and accepted. When a person understands why he feels this way, he is in a position to obtain some relief. The first step, therefore, is to utilize your God-given gift of reason for the analysis of your feelings. Moods of discouragement, together with the conditions and events that generate them, may be distorted and magnified by those who are tired and less resilient. One should ask himself just how real the basis for his feeling of depression is. A little bit of common sense analysis may initiate the journey back to hope and tranquility.

Many people who have been very active throughout their lives are subject to depression when they begin to feel useless. In our society, arbitrary retirement contributes to this problem. A man who has been one of the principals in a vast corporation suddenly finds himself to be nothing more than a tired old man. People who once came to him for his opinions come no more. He doesn't get any mail. Those who showed him great deference when he represented the corporation turn out to be fair-weather friends who can get along very well without him. Once he was sought after by every civic group, and now he must seek his own opportunities to help.

One of the greatest men I have known offered to work for his company without salary but was refused, even though he was in the best of health and better able to perform than anyone else in the company. This circumstance tends to bring on discouragement which, in turn, leads to depression, which can result in despair.

Mothers whose lives have been centered in their children may feel useless when the children are grown. Depression and loss of self-esteem are natural results of a feeling of uselessness. I have heard a mother say, "I was very happy when my children were little—they needed me then." The woman whose life is built around parenthood is in great demand for civic and recreational services while her children are with her. When the children are grown, however, she is no longer needed for the car pool; she is no longer in demand at the P.T.A. or the children's supervisory unit at the community center or the country club.

Her sense of uselessness is often comparable to the feeling of a retired executive. Even her church may not afford as much satisfaction as it did when her children were involved. If she tries to hold on to her grown children, she may spoil their lives. If she dominates her grandchildren, she becomes a pest. She is faced with the responsibility of finding other more appropriate activities. She has to move from one stage of human growth and development to another.

Our culture requires people to be good for something, and old people sometimes feel they are good for nothing. I have already mentioned the sense of worthlessness that very often comes from retirement or some inability to perform the useful tasks which once afforded the most satisfaction. Other causes of helplessness come from the realization that physical and intellectual powers have diminished. He who finds nothing important to do is certain to feel useless if he has been programmed for work and service.

The cure for feelings of worthlessness is readily available. All one needs is to do something worthwhile. And this old world is full of dire need. Kipling correctly described the value of every human being in his little verse "The Glory of the Garden":

There's not a pair of legs so thin
There is not a head so thick
There is not a hand so pale and weak
There is not a heart so sick
But it can find some piece of work
That's crying to be done
For the glory of God's garden
Glorifieth everyone.

The answer to all of this is that an older person must find useful activities. The service opportunities of volunteer organizations can be very helpful, but for many they lack a sense of genuine importance. Those who find a new sense of satisfaction in service to mankind are those who become involved in new careers. For many people, the sheer delight of being paid for a job well done lends a sense of legitimacy.

A merger brought on early retirement for one of my friends who had come to be president of a substantial industrial corporation. Through his ability as a financial manager (he was a certified public accountant), he had risen to the number one position. Upon retirement, he soon became a problem to himself. After some restless months, he found and accepted a post as comptroller for a large hospital system. The salary was a fraction of that received as president of the corporation, but he found more personal satisfaction in his new post than he had as a top corporate executive. He was doing something very useful, and this mobilized his remaining life. His skill in accounting, in the deployment of resources, in the formulation of financial procedures, in the areas of budgeting and auditing, all came into service—a part of the competence he had acquired through long study and experience. He moved from discouragement to a life of joy.

The opportunities for gainful employment by older people are more numerous than commonly supposed. Efforts to keep the jobs available just for the young prompt policies and legislation that rob retired persons of opportunities for service. This despite the fact that the old person may very well perform in a superior fashion because he has learned to go directly to the task at hand. The responsibility for finding appropriate employment lies with each of us. Some oldsters find ways of starting their own enterprises. Others find part-time work in their areas of competence. Some are able to fit into public service positions that can bring vocational fulfillment.

Volunteer service is not to be avoided. Old people have an obligation to perform it. For those who can find a sense of genuine usefulness in work for the church, the hospital, a community organization or a similar institution, there is help for humanity and satisfaction. Some older people find their way into politics. Opportunities, when they appear, bring with them the promise not only of some personal satisfaction and reward, but also of relief from the most persistent problem of the old—depression.

Play has a way of getting a person off his own hands so that feelings of discouragement are forgotten. A good active game of tennis is excellent therapy for a depressed mood. Golf is a jealous game which forbids a person to think about anything else. Less active games can relieve the pain of depression. A pleasant walk through a meadow, along a beach, or even down the street, is a great help when feelings of sadness blot out the sun. Recreation is very good medicine for the "blues."

Almost as devastating as depression is anxiety. Anxiety is a form of persistent fear. Fear is a very beneficial emotion when there is some genuinely frightening situation or threat. But when fear appears with no such stimulus, it becomes neurotic and can result in all sorts of psychosomatic difficulties. The ultimate fear of death is a big factor in the anxiety of many older people. To be sure, death will come, but cowering in its presence will only hasten its arrival. The sensible person must find enough interest in living to subordinate the fear of dying.

Fear of incapacitating disease is closely related to the fear of death. Even though many people say they prefer death to helplessness, when a situation arises in which a person suffers disablement, he still fights for life. The will to live is very strong and very persistent. If this were not the case, the race would have died out long ago. Fear of death can only make a bad situation worse.

One of the problems of old age is the lack of immunity to bacteria, viral infections, injuries, cerebral vascular accidents, problems of the intestinal tract, heart trouble, cancer, and all the other threats to health and life. When the dimension of fear is added, these threats are too often realized. The person who morbidly monitors his own health all the time is likely to wind up with the symptom he fears most. Naturally healthy people often become self-conscious when they read about the various diseases that come to human beings. My uncle called this tendency "a case of the hypos," his corruption of the term "hypochondriac."

The solution here is simple enough—face the fact that diseases can come, do whatever is possible to avoid them before they strike, and get medical help to find a cure if they do. Medical check-ups can be very reassuring. Few things prolong life as much as the reassurance which some patients feel when a thorough medical examination shows no physical basis for the presumed illness.

The fear from which anxiety springs is a deep and difficult emotion. It cannot be dispelled at will. Anxieties which were manageable in active middle years may get out of hand when physical energy ebbs and we have more time to fret. Many of my contemporaries complain of a generalized fear that something is going to happen. One friend, in fact, cringes at each curve when he is riding in an automobile, sure the car will crash. I have friends who sit in airplanes with white knuckles and a fixed stare. Some are afraid to travel because of their fear that illness will overtake them while they are abroad.

Grandparents are notable worriers. They tend to be uneasy about normal childish recklessness. The old grandfather in "Peter and the Wolf" is always sounding the alarm. This may be a good thing, within limits, but when it gets out of hand, it can be destructive both to the family and to the worrier. The person who gives in to anxieties may be completely paralyzed by them. It is perfectly true that something could happen to anybody, but the likelihood of it is negligible. Besides, constant worry doesn't help.

Some otherwise well and sensible people are scourged with foolish fears when money is involved. One of my contemporaries, who is a national celebrity with a very sound financial base, is under perpetual fear that something will happen to his financial security. He started out as a boy who experienced poverty and financial depression. He could never believe that the opulence of his productive years would last. Now that his career is in decline, he feels anxious lest he be drawn back into his childhood poverty.

Many oldsters worry about the world with as much gusto as some grandparents worry about their families. Anxiety, when it reaches such proportions as to threaten a person's happiness, requires proper attention. What can a person do?

Rigorous intellectual consideration of the emotional problem, to sort out the neurotic from the real, is the first step away from unwarranted anxiety. Sigmund Freud once said, "The intellect is weak, but very persistent." Rational attention will not correct an emotional problem, but it is very useful in the process of attempting to understand it. One of the great capabilities of human beings is their ability to take a responsible, objective look at their own feelings and difficulties. A little bit of reflection may provide a clue that might result in considerable relief from fear.

Everyone must find his own reassurance, even if what he comes up with is little better than a rabbit's foot. An intelligent course of action in money matters may reassure him he is not about to be left penniless. To give love to his family and receive love from them in return will lessen his fears that something is going to happen to them. Sensible action is the best possible protection against any kind of neurotic anxiety. Drive a car with caution and dispel the fear that an accident is about to happen. Riding in an airplane with pleasant companionship and reading, eating or carrying out of other activities can bring some relief from fear. There is no better cure for any kind of uneasiness than successful performance.

The person who is anxious about conditions in general cannot readily change the world, but he can, with attention, change his attitude toward it. I remember my father's story about the old Colorado rancher who was astonished to discover that the mountain still stood after William Jennings Bryan was defeated. There is a delightful little jingle which tells the story of how each age tends to fear that the world has fallen on evil times. Yet mankind has survived on this little planet—at least up until now:

> My granddad watched the world's worn cogs
>   and said we're going to the dogs.
> His granddad in a hut of logs
>   vowed things are going to the dogs.

His granddad in the Irish bogs
   swore things are going to the dogs.
His granddad dressed in caveman's togs
   said things are going to the dogs.
Now this is all I have to state,
   the dogs have had an awful wait.

Along with the problems of health, anxiety, discouragement and fear is the feeling of loneliness. One of my most distinguished friends, in his eightieth year, told me that the major inner problem for him was loneliness. He was a very great man who had influenced the destiny of the nation. As he approached eighty, however, his friends were mostly gone, and those who were living had no inclination to call on him for advice and counsel as had been their earlier custom. He had developed certain barriers with the members of his family over the fact that they rebelled against his very good advice. He had probably been a little too demanding, but here was a man whose last years were marked by a tragic sense of loneliness which drove out joy and brought on despair.

Old people need not be lonely. The most thriving organization in America appears to be The American Association of Retired People. Chapters are springing up all over the land. Old people are everywhere, and the organization's influence is substantial. The success of the movement derives in large part from the flight from loneliness. Active people need to feel a shoulder on the right and a shoulder on the left. The companionship of those who share the same feelings brings great satisfaction.

Loneliness is not difficult to manage if a person uses resourcefulness and initiative. With so many other lonely people in the world, all that is required is a friendly attitude, a telephone call and an effort to find friendship. The old person who feels so inadequate that he cannot be with other people without painful emotions of insecurity needs someone to help him get over his self-isolating and destructive problem.

In fact, the last cycle of life affords more opportunity for companionship than any other period. At the height of raising children or pursuing a career, a person lacks the time to cultivate friendships. The very young are too concerned with their own problems to develop the other's point of view, which is essential to friendship. Some of the most beautiful and tender ties in the world are found among aging cronies who enjoy one another.

People tend to exaggerate their difficulties as they grow older. Those who overindulge may get worse with age. Those who eat too much may compound their problems by growing too heavy and yielding to more overeating to escape feelings of loneliness, depression, or inadequacy. Many old people drink too much. Alcoholism is the major drug problem of our society. I have seen old people on the verge of intoxication angrily damning the young for using drugs, with no self-consciousness of their own activity as drug users. Moderation is the hallmark of wisdom, and wisdom is the glory of maturity. The person who has developed an alcohol problem does well to get help. Alcoholics Anonymous has been one of the most successful therapies in our era. It has the advantage of providing companionship in addition to the procedures for control. New medical aids appear with each session of the research institutes that deal with this particular drug problem. A combination of resolve, companionship and medical help can solve this persistent and debilitating problem.

Among other difficulties that face retired people is the human inclination to keep on fighting old battles, even though victory or defeat no longer has any meaning. Many people worry over slights, injustices, embarrassments that occurred many years ago. Some past struggles in the office or in the family may be clearly remembered with so much ego involvement that the encounter is repeated inwardly, constantly.

The human memory is somewhat analogous to a tape recorder. When some sight, sound or smell turns on the switch, the whole episode runs through the mind. The old person, once again, becomes an active participant in a situation that seems to matter greatly, even though it is long forgotten by others, some of whom may be already dead.

The person who feels he was wronged in some conflict which involved his feelings of dignity and self-respect may find himself rehearsing what he should have said and what he should have done, even though he is at this moment an old man walking on a beach. Some passing experience has awakened the old feelings of anger, hurt, shame and injustice. Old military officers often fight their earlier battles. Old athletes replay the ballgame. Retired business executives imagine they have managed to fire the people they could not get rid of at the time. Poignant experiences of youth which involved humiliation, exposure, rejection, shame and guilt may come back to spoil a pleasant afternoon beside a tranquil lake. The age of wisdom requires that a person commune with his own past to work out an agreement of peace with amnesty for those who have done him wrong. This may be fairly easy to do, anyway, since many may be dead.

The passing years may loosen the grip one has on his behavior. Self-discipline comes, in part, from colleagues and companions of the middle years. When these are no longer near, a person may relax and grow fat, for instance. The concentration involved in limiting one's intake of food is far greater than most people imagine. Wiry and skinny people who can eat anything without accumulating avoirdupois are very impatient with those of us who eat an extra sandwich and gain two pounds. Some old people find it easy to cut down on consumption of food, but others find in the delight of feasting compensation for what they have been deprived of by advancing years.

Dieting is indicated for almost everybody, but especially for those of us who have passed the magic age of seventy. Mahatma Gandhi overdid it, but his self-discipline was in the right direction. A person is much more likely to die from overeating than from starvation. Understanding the elements of nutrition is not only good sense but can very well be fun. One need not become a food faddist and a bore in the process. God save us from these!

Self-discipline is important for other areas, such as management of time and activities. Old people are said to become childish, and many of them illustrate this by doing only those things they enjoy and conveniently forgetting to do those things which they do not like. Those who like to play, play too much. Those who like to work, work too much. Those who like to sit, sit too much; and those who like to drink, drink too much. Most of all, those who like to talk, talk too much. Every oldster needs to budget his time with the same rigor and care required to budget his money and his calories. This need not be a laborious process with a flare of trumpets, but it does require the application of common sense to the time at one's disposal before the final evening comes on.

An aging person feels pain here and there, and with it a variety of feelings that indicate bodily malfunction. The lore of grandparents includes dyspepsia, rheumatism and gout. There are many others much more subtle, and some of them are unmentionable—or at least should be.

But the person who becomes preoccupied with health can develop into an outrageous bore. Complaining and whining people are never in strong demand. Those who are deeply in love with their own pains and symptoms are on the way to rejection. Nothing can spoil a greeting more quickly than for a person to answer in full detail when someone innocently asks, "How are you?" A good honest answer is enough without undue elaboration. The bodily processes that are fascinating to the person who experiences them are not of major concern or interest to the casual listener.

Some old people are inclined to withdraw from society. The death of a spouse may cause the survivor to become reclusive. Some physical impairment may seem so enormous that being with people seems too much of a burden and too much exposure. Guilt-ridden people may try to hide from the public. The old person who stands up to life has learned how to master the inclination to withdraw. Everybody feels an occasional urge to resign from the human race, but those with courage meet the world head-on and live out their lives with a certain amount of charm, delight and joy.

Old people are social beings the same as young people. The age of wisdom is a beautiful time for companionship. Picture the older Emerson and the older Carlyle sitting in silence before a fire for an entire evening before one arose to say good night and express pleasure in the evening of fellowship.

Self-centeredness is a most persistent problem at any age, but it shows up more when a person is plagued with other difficulties, such as ill health, withdrawal, loneliness and depression. I spent a day with some of my companions of former years on a recent occasion and was impressed with the fact that each one of us might just as well have been alone. There was limited awareness, a modicum of communication, very little appreciation for one another and a great deal of self-centered conversation. All were annoyed when another was speaking. With his mind firmly fixed on what he had to say, each person found it difficult to await an opportunity to break in. This was not a typical collection of my contemporaries, but it describes too many associations of people. The fact that many of them could not hear very well contributed to the problem, but the major difficulty was that each person was preoccupied with his own little affairs. Even this was not enough for these egocentrics. There was the general expectation that everybody else ought to be primarily interested in the same little world.

The cultivation of an other-regarding point of view is a lifelong experience, but seventy is a good time to start if it hasn't been started earlier. A person learns to empathize with his companions by deliberate awareness of their needs and interests. The art of careful listening is beautiful at any age, but it becomes a venerable citizen better than his fame or fortune.

Many physicians learn the art of complete identification with the needs and concerns of their patients. Counselors must learn this art or they are not counselors. A truly effective parent feels the concern of a child in his own heart. After a person becomes aware of the feelings of his associates and learns how to listen and speak to their needs, he can begin to project himself into their points of view. He can begin to see the world through another pair of eyes and to experience the world through another person's feelings and ideas. This sensitivity enriches life for everybody. Conversation becomes alive when people have developed the other-regarding point of view—the hallmark of true wisdom.

Dr. Menninger has pointed out that the most persistent dread of most people is that of being left alone. To be abandoned is one of the most frightening experiences known. Self-centered people even blame friends and spouses who have died for leaving them—alone. Thackeray, lion of the literary world that he was, said one day, "Most of us are very lonely in this world. Any of you who have friends, cling to them and thank God." The fear of being alone is most readily managed when one has enough courage to face the issue and enough resourcefulness to relieve the pain.

I have many friends who have learned how to live very happily alone. They have learned how to overcome the fear by self-acceptance, self-recognition and interest in other people. Those who make the most of the necessity know how to cultivate friendships, accept kindness, entertain friends and generally prove themselves desirable companions.

There is a perceptive verse in the Bible, which says, "Perfect love driveth out fear." When a person has learned to love other people, and to love himself, he has gained mastery over that persistent fear of being left alone. It is the fortunate fact that those who find peace in being alone are spared enervating loneliness.

RENEWAL AND PERSONAL RELATIONSHIPS

My friend Norman Vincent Peale wrote, *The Power of Positive Thinking*, and the idea swept the country. Many of us in academics were afraid that the good and revered clergyman had proposed "positive thinking" as a sort of self-hypnotic spell that might ignore the substance and jagged truths of life. This was not the case. Dr. Peale had a solid point. The positive attitude makes a tremendous difference in life.

My theory of renewal in later years, however, is more than the power of positive thinking. It is a careful observation of the actual changes that occur in people when they can provide the conditions that enable them to "mount up with wings as eagles." The positive attitude is important, but it can persist only if a person gets a whole new image of aging. A positive attitude toward the old-car theory will not keep it from breaking down. The most optimistic person in the world cannot overcome his dire expectations if he thinks of himself as an old tree, ready to totter. My personal experience shows that my mind, my feelings and my body are literally renewed by these surges of power and ability that have come in later life. I see the same reaction among some of my friends, even though they may not be fully aware of what is happening.

One of the principal factors in finding the true joy and meaning of later life is found in the way we relate to people. Love and friendship are the stuff of life at any age, but they are absolutely essential for the renewed person in later life. My attitude toward my friends is different now that I have discovered the surge of the sixties and a confident outlook for the seventies and beyond. I am much more aware of the needs and interests of people around me. I believe it is fair to say that young people tend to be more self-centered, although they differ widely in this respect. Sensitivity to the needs of others advances with years. But a very self-centered youth will probably be a very self-centered old person and sometimes a person can be self-centered while young and become very sensitive to other people as the years advance. I have noticed something of this inclination in my own life and in the lives of those around me.

Modern knowledge has brought no magic to interpersonal relationships, but the psychiatrists and sociologists have come up with some very striking observations about how people manage to get along with one another. These principles do not change just because someone understands his own renewal. There is still the need for patient adjustment and readjustment in the stresses of life. The following observations are based on my own experience and wide reading. I present them here as a set of principles and observations that might be useful to anyone who wishes to make the most of his renewed life by practicing the high art of getting along with the people around him.

The wisdom years afford an opportunity for a person to get along with his family and friends. If he hasn't learned the art of human relations before he reaches seventy, he had better go to work on it posthaste. The sad fact is that abrasive and prickly personalities are usually unaware of their own foibles. A pig does not know he is greedy, an ox does not know he is patient, and a church mouse does not know he is poor. If a person finds himself short on friends and long on enemies, he needs to take a double look in a mirror. The art of getting along with people is essential to our crowded world. Older people need friends and happy companionship, both of which are dependent upon one's ability to live in peace and harmony with his fellow human beings. A dash of charm makes life even better.

The hard work of life's middle years tends to relieve the aggressive energy which each person possesses. I once knew a woman who loved to beat rugs on the theory that after she had thoroughly beaten the rugs, she could be decent to her husband. Slights and insults are soon forgotten if a person is extremely busy. Work and play alike are effective means of handling aggressive emotions of anger and hostility. A retired person can still work and play enough to relieve his emotions, but it may require some conscious effort on his part. One of my friends leaves his apartment and jogs when he finds himself snapping at his wife. He is a shrewd psychologist, and his wife is a fortunate woman.

Hurt feelings, feelings of inadequacy, feelings of jealousy or anger, feelings even of hate, come to everybody. The human mind is a resourceful rationalizer. Instead of accepting the fact that these emotions are the common lot of humankind, our minds deceive us into thinking that we have been treated unjustly or that somebody else is to blame. When I was very young, I was disposed to blame people for being jealous. One of my friends, a very bright lawyer named Rice Tilley, said "Don't blame these people, Perry; they can't help that." People can learn how to handle such emotions, even though their presence is unavoidable when a whole lifetime of attitudes has been written into a personality. The same principle holds for all our emotional responses. To be sure, other people are blameworthy on occasion, but the inner reactions are our own. When we are hurt or angered, we are responsible, even though someone else may be the culprit.

When a person accepts responsibility for his own emotional feelings and his own attitudes, he has taken the first step toward getting along with other people. This does not mean that he has learned to comply with the aggressive wishes of someone else. It means he has recognized his own part in a two-way transaction. Armed with the sense of his own emotional predicament, he can begin to deal with the inevitable problems in human relationships as a skillful fencer deals with his opponent, knowing full well that his plight depends on himself. His opponent is the given factor in the situation.

138

Getting along with people is primarily a problem in awareness. Nobody is worthy of friendship unless he can look at the world through other people's eyes, listen through other people's ears, and feel the world through other people's needs and concerns. Human relations depend on regard for one another's point of view. This trait can be learned. As a matter of fact, only those who have learned it have it. Concern for the other person is about the most appealing characteristic of the wisdom years. Young people can be forgiven for being shockingly unaware of anybody else, but old people ought to know better. This kind of awareness comes from observing, listening, pondering and imagining. Only the person who is interested in his fellow human beings will develop this art. The heart of the law and the gospel is to love God with all one's heart, soul, mind and strength, and one's neighbor as oneself. This commandment is based on the problem of human awareness and concern.

One of my friends wrote a book on the causes of failure in marriage. He discovered that neither money nor sex, as many suppose, is the principal cause, but rather, ego differences. A woman loves a man in terms of her image of what he should be and what he can do for her. A man loves a woman in terms of his ego interests, his image of what she should be and what she can do for him. When they mutually find out that these ego interests are incompatible, the storm breaks.

Every human being has this problem in regard to his human relations. People are what they are, not what you wish them to be. Not only must the person who has friends accept himself as one with attitudes of bias and feelings of inadequacy, jealousy, fear or aggressiveness, but he must accept other people as possessing these same qualities—perhaps even to a worse degree. Adjustment of these ego differences is never easy.

Friendship cannot be made; it grows. One cannot grow tomatoes by pulling on the vines. One can encourage the growth of tomatoes by appropriate cultivation and by providing the water, nourishment and other conditions required. The growth of the plant, however, is beyond human control. Friendship is comparable. The expression "make friends" is unfortunate. A person can provide the appropriate conditions and cultivate a friendship, but that cherished friendship is a gift of God.

One of the prime conditions that encourage friendship, second only to the other-regarding point of view which I have mentioned, is a common interest. Two people looking at each other are headed for an ego clash. When they look together at something better and more important than both of them, friendship begins to grow. People who work together, play together, or are paired and accidentally placed close to each other tend to like each other if conditions are favorable.

The greatest friendships of this world have come out of common enterprises involving victory, defeat, suffering and triumph. Antoine de Saint-Exupéry, in his *Flight to Arras,* wrote about the men who came back from the rain of terror and flak through which they had flown in their bombing missions: "They had earned the right to sit down together as friends." Persons who have faced common dangers, common fears and common foes become identified with each other. This ego identification is involved in all human relationships. It was nicely expressed by the Chinese poet who said of her dead lover, "It was as if part of me had died."

The ambiguities of life are such that not everybody can be a friend of everybody. Some people dislike each other and that is that. The frayed jingle bears repeating:

"I do not like thee, Dr. Fell,
The reason why I cannot tell;
But one sure thing I know full well:
I do not like thee, Dr. Fell."

Most people, however, can respond to that beautiful remark of Will Rogers, "I never met a man I didn't like,"—that is if there is time enough, patience enough and sufficient inclination. Old people have time to be friends, and friendship is essential to a long life.

There is a certain order in human relations. When we first meet a person, we tend to respond with enthusiasm. The new neighbor, the new golf companion, the new manager of the neighborhood store and the new friend we met at a dinner party elicit a response of enthusiasm. We find we have interests in common—perhaps even dislike the same things. I know of two people who became fast friends because neither one likes gravy! I have watched my students develop quick cliquish friendships on the basis of this first blush of acquaintance. But stage one soon ends.

Stage two comes when each becomes aware that the other has faults. This is another way of saying that the other person does not conform to my inner image of him. Nobody can exactly fit the standards expected of him by another person. Each has his own background, his own concerns, his own ego interests and his own purposes. When these clash, disenchantment comes. Irritations abound. Enthusiasm gives way to questioning, perhaps even to doubt. Many friendships break up at this point. Only patient understanding and mutual acceptance can continue beyond the disillusioning shock and irritations of what the person says, does and is.

The third stage, when and if it is reached, is acceptance and understanding. When I can love my fellow man even though he is something very different than I thought and wish him to be, then I have enriched my own life and enlarged my own horizons. Persons who truly accept each other, faults and all, can become friends. Sometimes the virtues are harder to forgive than the faults. But interpersonal relations grow and become integrated as people increase their ability to accept, respect and forgive virtues and vices alike.

I came across these three stages of interpersonal relations when I was a student in graduate school. That distinguished scholar-lecturer William Ernest Hocking was a guest teacher who discussed these principles as pertinent to the relationships between nations, communities, interest groups and other human situations—as well as the relationships between individuals. I have long observed the ways in which people interact and have concluded that Professor Hocking's formula is both correct and practical. I have seen prickly relationships smoothed, marriages saved, enmities dispelled and old wounds healed by the insight and practice of Professor Hocking's formula. I recommend it to all.

There is an old Pennsylvania Dutch maxim quoted from Goethe: "To love and to be loved is the greatest thing in the world." This is not only true but crucial to anyone who wants to prolong his life. One of my psychologist friends performed a careful experiment and discovered that dogs who are loved are healthier and live longer. My own observations and experience lead me to believe that nothing is more beneficial to health and wellbeing than the joy of giving and receiving love. The kindly expression, the warm handclasp, the word of endearment can quicken the pulses of grandparents as readily as those of children. Ripened love between an old couple requires expression both in word and action. Loving and loved old people not only live longer but are more fun.

A person's relationship to family and close friends requires honesty, understanding, patience and a great deal of kindness. More superficial relationships can survive on cheerfulness and a smile.

Many people give the impression of hostility without intending to do so. Preoccupation with pain, some problem at hand or some reflection on a past event may result in grim lines in the face which signal combat. The older person does well to remember the importance of a smile. Considerable psychological research results in the conclusion that nothing signals a warm and friendly personality as much as a smile. Anything can be overdone, of course. But the face which lights up when an acquaintance appears or someone performs a courtesy encourages friendly and pleasant human relations.

The art of expressing appreciation and gratitude is most important in the fret and jar of human affairs. A kindly word of praise may lift the sagging spirit of a friend or win the attention of someone who would become a friend. Pleasant people are always in demand. Even dour people can learn to be pleasant if they are willing to work at it. Look for and expect the best in people. Honor them and mention their achievements, their appearance, their kindnesses. The late Edgar DeWitt Jones changed the attitudes of the people in any room he entered. There was a quality of style, cheer and greatness about him. Almost anyone can develop sufficient radiance to lighten up a dark room. Sales people dearly love to see some customers walk into a store. The grumbling, complaining, whining sourpuss is welcome nowhere.

Between the casual acquaintance and the intimate relationship of a family, one must frequently deal with people who present particular problems. Relationship with an aggressive person, for example, requires either subservience, a means of circumvention or a battle. Some people are aggressive by long habit and experience. I remember one member of the Bethany College faculty who was quite aggressive and explained it by saying that her sister was nice to people and didn't seem to get anywhere. The best way of dealing with a person who is obnoxious is to avoid dealing with him. If the situation is not that drastic, a person can learn to accept aggressiveness the same as he learns to accept any limitations in others. This does not mean surrender. He who learns how to accept aggression without anger or subservience may find a pleasant relationship with an aggressive person who is lonely.

An even more perplexing problem is dealing with jealousy, whether it be within oneself or some companion. Rational analysis has little influence on strong feelings such as jealousy. Try to accept such feelings and attempt to find a way to control the impulses to flight or destruction. Some envious people find comfort in pointing out the flaws in the personality and appearance of the person who brings on their feelings of jealous anger and resentment. This is not very satisfactory. Everybody has flaws and attempting to point them out may bring retaliation. A much better procedure is to find some outlet in work or play to channel the emotional impulses. At the same time, strive to build up your self confidence to the extent that jealousy is unnecessary.

When the jealous person is on the attack, however, the problem is more difficult. Some persons are jealous but are not destructive with it. One can often relieve the pressure by emphasizing admirable traits and by attempting to bring out the best in the jealous person. With growing self-esteem the feelings of jealousy may subside. In my long professional career, I have suffered at the hands of jealous people who have tried defamation, ridicule, false accusations and almost everything short of physical violence. I have outlived them all with no scars on the outside and only a few on the inside. I have tried to be gentle and resourceful in dealing with them, up to a point; but when a situation required action I have been willing to defend. There is no easy cure for this predicament, but frank recognition of its existence can suggest effective methods of response.

Insecure people create problems in human relationships. The person who always has hurt feelings may cause his friends to treat him with great respect—a condition which appeals to him strongly. I remember reporting to the chairman of my philosophy department that he had inadvertently hurt the feelings of one of my colleagues in the department. He smiled wisely and said, "Do you think he wished to have his feelings hurt?" I concluded that his diagnosis was correct.

I have learned never to worry about losing friends because I have hurt their feelings unintentionally. As long as we are worthy of each other, the friendship will not be lost. I try to avoid hurting anyone unnecessarily. Chesterfield's definition of a gentleman as "A person who never unintentionally hurts anyone's feelings," is a very high standard. I have known a few people who were not only thin-skinned, but had practically no skin at all. They could even twist a compliment into a slight. What does one do in dealing with such people? The answer is to do your very best to show concern for their feelings and sensitivities, but beyond that, to live your life and trust God to preserve the friendship.

The consummate egotist is another difficult companion. There is a charming story about the man who emerged from some psychological counsel to say, "You know, before I had these interviews, I was the most egotistical and pretentious person you can imagine. Now, since I have gone through this program, I am the nicest man in town." Egotism is born of insecurity. The boy in doubt of his own power is always picking a fight to prove he can whip somebody. The best way to deal with the egotist is to allow him enough reassurance to avoid destructive outbreaks of speech or behavior. The insecure person becomes combative when he is threatened. It costs little to reinforce the sagging self-confidence of another person, even if that self-confidence takes a somewhat pretentious turn. But when egotist meets egotist, the fur flies.

Dr. Eric Berne points out the difficulty in dealing with sulks. He defines a sulk as a person whose childhood conflict with a parent surfaces later as a determination to do nothing that other people expect of him. The person who is never prepared, always late, disposed to complain at everything, unhappy and resentful of authority presents a difficult social problem. Within limits, one would do well to accept a certain amount of non-compliance with accepted norms. A permissive person may deprive him of the joy of rebellion, but may also, on occasion, improve his performance and promote his social tranquility.

To classify all sorts of people that one meets in the golden years is quite impossible. Everyone is a unique creation with his own eccentricities, inclinations, habits and behavior patterns. I have mentioned a few personality types because of their frequent recurrence. You meet these people in the leisure village, in the rest home, on the play field, on a world cruise or in the neighborhood association. Everyone has learned certain ways to deal with people. But everyone can improve on his performance by thoughtful attention, resourcefulness and self-denial.

Perhaps the most important factor in human relations is style. Each unique person has the privilege and responsibility of being himself. The person who develops a life around integrity, honor and human kindness is better armed for the enjoyment of friendship than the person who is blessed with handsome features and little spiritual substance.

Physical appearance attracts people at once, but character attracts people forever. Those people who have learned how to live serenely through difficult times, who have come to accept their own limitations of health, wealth and ability, and who have learned to walk with dignity and pride bring happiness not only to themselves, but to others. They have learned from Matthew Arnold the truth of that great closing line, "Resolve to be thyself and know that he who finds himself loses his misery."

Grudges have no place in the golden years. People of achievement accumulate enemies as the busy years take their toll. Difficult decisions, bold actions, clash of wills, conflicts of purpose bring on enmity. A few enemies are inevitable for a strong and active person. As the last stage of life begins, however, the wise person works at the high moral principle of forgiveness with a new dedication. An active executive can afford a few enemies, and this is fortunate, because he is sure to have one or two. But when the fire burns down, one can no longer afford them. The energy required by resentful feelings is needed for survival.

The wise and gentle command of Jesus becomes inperative: "Love your enemies; do good unto them that despitefully use you." These words were spoken for the good of the person and not for the good of the enemies. Enemies may not deserve forgiveness, but the wise person will forgive them anyhow—this for his own good. There is nothing more pathetic than an old person who hates his resentful way through the last years of his life. He has missed the tranquillity and peace which the last stage offers. Moreover, he has shown himself to be less than wise.

My long life has brought its share of struggle and difference. Nobody can manage business enterprises, churches and colleges without collecting some enemies. Now I am faced with the problem of forgiving them. Some of the people who tried to destroy me and my whole professional career are dead. The fact that an enemy dies does not bring forgiveness, even though it diminishes the intensity of the feelings and removes the reason for combat. Wise old people forgive their adversaries, dead or alive.

When I find myself reflecting on the past struggles in which I was severely threatened, I pause to consider how that struggle must have seemed to my opponent. This awakens feelings of understanding and sympathy which can, with time and love, become compassion. When I have managed to feel genuine compassion, it becomes possible to move toward forgiveness. A person may even come to feel the genuine affection that might have continued, had the conflict been resolved without enmity. My own resolve and my advice to my contemporaries is to turn our enemies into friends as speedily as possible in order that we may "not let the sun go down on our wrath." The mantle of charity is big enough to cover the conflicts of the past.

What then becomes of the aggressive energy once needed for struggle and defense? It can be invested in work, play and survival. Even spectator sports require enough emotion to reduce the hostility. The battles against ignorance, error and evil need all of the aggressive energy we can muster. Wisdom does not deny us the thrill of combat. It simply redirects our battle plan to the end that we strike out against worthy contemporary opponents rather than the diminishing adversaries of the long ago.

SOARING OVER THE VALLEY

R enewal does not deny the reality of death. Sooner or later every life must come to an end. Renewal means that life can be glorious and triumphant before death comes. It certainly tends to delay the arrival, but the time comes when our earthly pilgrimage must end. My old friend R. Livingston Ireland says, "May the grim reaper catch up with you with your boots on." Death does not hold the terror for a renewed person that it does for one who is resigned and discouraged.

In my long life, I have stood by the bedside of many dying people. Those who had found true renewal faced death in a glorious and triumphant fashion. They were able to "mount up with wings" even when they were all set to soar over the valley of the shadow.

One of my scholarly friends of long ago called the fear of death "the disease of Europe." And he spoke of some Oriental cultures in which there is little, if any, terror connected with dying. We have surrounded the last of life with so many superstitions and terrors that the natural appears to be the horrible. I do not say that death is a welcome visitor. The will to live is about the most basic attitude of a normal human being. I do say that the great trilogy of "faith, hope and love" can lift the renewed person above the terror and despair which may invite an early demise. Renewal means a new attitude toward death itself.

The late John Cooper Powys argued that the most comforting thought when one is discouraged is death itself. His elaboration indicated that when a person thinks about death and its gravity, he can only be relieved of his lesser cares, worries and depression. While I have found this idea interesting, I do not share this inverted comfort which comes from thinking about death. My own experience is that a person should follow his natural inclination to stay alive by enjoying every minute until the inevitable occurs. Maurice Chevalier captured the whimsical mood when he said, in response to the question, "How do you like being old?": "When I consider the alternative, it is just great!" He held with Powys.

A much more effective sentiment, however, is in the old toast which goes, "May you live all the days of your life."

Robert Browning had this fine sentiment when he wrote of death in 1861:

Fear death?—to feel the fog in my throat,
  The mist in my face,
When the snows begin, and the blasts denote
  I am nearing the place,
The power of the night, the press of the storm,
  The post of the foe;

Where he stands, the Arch Fear in a visible form,
Yet the strong man must go.
For the journey is done and the summit attained,
And the barriers fall,
Though a battle's to fight ere the guerdon be gained,
The reward of it all.
I was ever a fighter, so—one fight more,
The best and the last!
I would hate that death bandaged my eyes, and
forebode,
And bade me creep past.
No! let me taste the whole of it, fare like my peers
The heroes of old,
Bear the brunt, in a minute pay glad life's arrears
Of pain, darkness and cold.
For sudden the worst turns the best to the brave,
The black minute's at end,
And the elements' rage, the fiend-voices that rave,
Shall dwindle, shall blend,
Shall change, shall become first a peace out of pain,
Then a light, then thy beast,
O thou soul of my soul! I shall clasp thee again,
And with God be the rest![1]

Death is the ultimate test of a person's faith. The mere thought of it forces one back on his more elemental inclinations and his cosmic commitments.

When Rudyard Kipling was near death the nurse asked him what he wanted, and, with the simplicity of a child, he said, "I want my heavenly father." How many people have been sustained by the serene and gentle comfort of the 23rd Psalm.

The fourteenth chapter of John, which begins, *"In my Father's house are many mansions"* has brought comfort to a multitude approaching the end of life. How many times have I cradled in that great scripture, *"The eternal God is thy refuge and underneath are the everlasting arms."* If the re-

---

1 "Prospice" in *From Beowulf to Thomas Hardy,* Robert Shafer, ed., Vol. II (New York: Doubleday, Doran & Co., 1929), p. 533.

newed person would "mount up with wings as eagles" to soar over the valley of the shadow of death, he would do well to renew his faith along with his mind and body; for when the time comes, the faith of one's childhood comes back to comfort and sustain. I have written my own personal testimony as follows:

FAITH FOR THE FUTURE

As I live through the experiences of retirement, pain from tic douloureux, a minor impairment in hearing and some of the inevitable problems of the late sixties, I meet with occasional moods of discouragement. Sometimes these moods get a little bit out of hand and approach despair. I have discovered that many of my contemporaries have similar experiences. I have discovered that others are subject to moments of disgust and despair but are unable to face the facts—they pretend they are just having a beautiful time. Great expectations for oneself, like life itself, must diminish and eventually conclude.

Many of my friends find consolation and help in religion as the shadows lengthen and the problems multiply. This is my experience as well. From childhood on, religion has afforded great personal satisfaction. I found Bible stories fascinating from the time I could first read. I participated in church events when I was still a child. I felt no alienation from the church such as seems common to many young people of college age with whom I have worked in the last decade or two. The fatherhood of God and the brotherhood of man is a basic assumption of my entire life. In moments of joy and celebration, I have found meaning and additional satisfaction in the heritage of faith. In times of loss, anxiety, disappointment and bereavement, I have found comfort and courage.

It is only natural, therefore, that my faith has increased rather than diminished with advancing years. I have examined the basic doctrines of the Judeo-Christian faith with the same philosophical rigor which I have applied to the works of Plato and the writings of Adam Smith. I am convinced that a student who fails to learn anything about the Bible is more diminished than if he fails to read Shakespeare and Marcus Aurelius. Dante and Milton are incomprehensible without some study of the holy scriptures. Some of the most cherished music springs from the deep devotion of faith. Bach, for instance, was more interested in religion than he was in art; it was his faith that produced the greatest music. Michelangelo would have been little more than ordinary had it not been for his religious commitment. The architects of Chartres Cathedral built mansions of faith which far surpassed their handsome and durable masterpiece in stone.

Religion is far more than intellectual. It is far more than emotional. It involves the most ultimate commitment of an entire life. For that reason, my personal Christian faith is more cherished with advancing years. When pain is more than I can bear, I lean back on the everlasting arms. When problems are too complex to manage, I find additional insight and strength in the divine realm which overarches and supercedes the human. Religion is the best medicine for disgust and despair. It can be of great help in times of pain. It is more effective than the various secular attempts at meditation or rituals of self-improvement and self-help.

When I was very young, I was excited about religion as a source of social reform. No doubt this was an appropriate investment of my time and talent. With passing years, I have found that I have served as secretary of many lost causes which now seem well lost. I have no quarrel with those who are inspired to all sorts of social action by virtue of religious commitment. From the standpoint of my present state of maturity, however, I find more interest in the broader aspects of faith which deal with great moral principles rather than ephemeral issues. I have earned the right to a certain detachment from some of the hot little frenzies of my young days. As I write to those who are growing old, I share this brief summary of what I call a faith for the future.

A vital faith in God enables an older person to rise above the exigencies of his own existence. The overarching commitment of religion lifts him above history to the realm of the eternal. The fret and jar of everyday life—with its problems of health, money, moods and disappointments—tend to preoccupy us with the present. Overconcern with this civilization and this era blinds us to the awesome and reassuring fact of eternity. A vital faith involves an abiding sense of the eternal. Nothing could be more comforting as one begins to round out his career. Consider for example, that great ninetieth Psalm:

Lord, thou hast been our dwelling place
in all generations.
Before the mountains were brought forth,
or ever thou hadst formed the earth
and the world, even from everlasting
to everlasting, thou art God.

Religion is also a love affair between God and man. When Jesus was asked to name the great commandment, he said:

Thou shalt love the Lord thy God with all
thy heart, and with all thy soul,
and with all thy mind.
This is the first commandment.
And the second is like unto it, Thou
shalt love thy neighbour as thyself.
On these two commandments hang all the law
and the prophets.

Matt. 22: 36-40

To love God with all the heart implies a complete emotional commitment. A person dominated with this one great feeling of devotion can face any issue without terror or defeat. To love God with all the soul has reference to the singleness of purpose which was in the mind of General William Booth when he said, "Reservation is the damnation of consecration." To love God with all the mind brings the human intellect into service. One of the most neglected aspects of the Judeo-Christian tradition is the intellectual love of God. Too many people have been content with feelings and deeds without rigorous thought. To love God with all one's strength refers to the conduct of life. An unshakable faith is best exemplified by a worthy and honorable life. To love one's neighbor as oneself is an inevitable consequence to the all-out love of God.

The person who has a sense of the eternal and who is enthralled with "God, the father almighty" has a sense of forgiveness. Forgiveness is the dominant theme of religion and the hope of humanity that we might gain release from feelings of guilt. Guilt is a destructive emotion even though most everybody deserves to feel guilty. The incarnation, life, crucifixion and resurrection of Christ constitute a study in human guilt and its redemption through atonement and forgiveness.

One summer long ago when I was in London I made my way to the City Temple where Leslie Weatherhead was the preacher. It was a lovely evening as the sun had just fallen beyond the skyline of the venerable buildings. The church was already full. There was a hush of expectancy as Dr. Weatherhead stood up to preach. His first words were, "The forgiveness of sins is probably the greatest message of the church." I heard with interest and excitement his thoughtful sermon with its engaging illustrations. The quiet hymn was sung, the benediction given and we walked out into the soft, English evening. There was a new glory around old London town. I felt somehow cleansed and more worthy in the eyes of God and man. Best of all, I felt somewhat more acceptable to myself.

I find consolation in that dramatic insight of a summer evening sermon even though the message had been available to me all the time in the Prophets and in the Gospels. I had been reminded of forgiveness each time I had been in church, almost every Sunday; yet it came home to me in a striking fashion on that evening long ago when I needed reassurance, and the meaning lingers after four decades. An aging person either learns how to deal with the problem of guilt or he must suffer self-destructive torments. Coleridge had this problem in mind when he wrote of the ancient mariner with a dead albatross fastened around his neck. When the sky was lead and the air was still there was no hope for the becalmed mariner until he began to feel compassion and love. A sense of forgiveness followed and the albatross dropped from his neck.

Religion lifts man above his inner thoughts and beliefs. It also lifts him above his public conduct and his interactions with other people. The private order of life deals with personal convictions, a private sense of beauty, secret loves and deep reflections such as one experiences in art, worship and contemplation. The public order of life has to do with the social activities of a human being. This is the world of economics, recreation, conversation and every such public aspect of human behavior. Religion, however, deals with an order of life which is beyond society.

A faith tends to become unshakable when a person realizes that God's universe goes on even though civilizations come and go. The life of man is relatively brief, but the life of God is forever. In Tennyson's fine words:

Our little systems have their day;
They have their day and cease to be;
They are but broken lights of thee,
And thou, O Lord, art more than they.

When this idea becomes a part of us, the framework and meaning of life begin to emerge. A person can give up the egocentric notion that his death is the end of the world. He begins to see his own life as an important part of a much larger existence. Paul was attempting to describe this mood when he said, "It is no longer I that live, but Christ lives in me." An unshakable faith is a very personal conviction. It is rough hewn out of experience. It cannot be transmitted by another person. It is a gift of God which is available only to that person who is prepared to receive it. It carries with it a sense of triumph over all the difficulties of life, including even death.

Belief in immortality is the ultimate article of a religious faith. It is a conviction that death is just one more event in the divine play. It is not a matter of logical proof and scientific data—impressive as these efforts have been in recent years. A belief in life after death is an extension of belief in God.

It is best illustrated by the story of a little boy who wandered down the aisle of a great westbound passenger train when the nation was still young and a westward journey was still an adventure. An old westerner with a large watchchain from which a gold nugget was swinging smiled at the little boy and in his blunt way said, "Sonny, where are you going?" The little boy smiled and answered, "I'm going out west." The blunt man said, "Where out west?" The boy answered, "I don't know." In a teasing mood, the man said, "You are a great one. You're going west and you don't know where you are going." The little boy said, "My father is here in the car and he knows." Perhaps something of this kind was what the good Lord had in mind when he said, "Unless you become as a little child, you cannot enter into the Kingdom of Heaven."

Churches and synagogues are the institutional expression of religious faith. They exemplify such cherished doctrines as forgiveness of sins and a sense of the eternal. They touch our little human lives with immortality by re-affirming our faith in life after death. They surround the exigencies of life with divine celebration which provides a whole new dimension of meaning.

Many people talk about having profound religious faith without any inclination to participate in a congregation. Personal religion without any institutional affiliation is possible, but difficult. One might as well talk about justice without courts or education without schools as to talk about religion without churches or synagogues. Individual religion can be lonely without a shoulder on the right and a shoulder on the left which provide a sense of community in the worship of God.

The practice of worship keeps alive a sense of the holy. When Isaiah was in the Temple, he saw the Lord high and lifted up. This removed the penitent prophet from his self-centered impotence. He became truly a child of God with vision, imagination and a plan. When God said, "Whom shall I send and who will go for us?" Isaiah was afraid and smitten with feelings of inadequacy. He only cried out, "Woe is me for I am a man of unclean lips and I dwell among a people of unclean lips." An angel took a coal from the altar and touched his lips. Then he could answer, "Here am I, Lord, send me."

Across the rolling centuries comes the repeated reenactment of this drama which restores quavering individuals to the unshakable faith of their forbears. The ways of worship vary from high liturgy to intimate folksiness or even to the practice of corporate silence. Whatever the chosen manner of expressing devotion to God the Father Almighty, there is the joy and meaning of hymns, prayers, sermons and ecclesiastical art expressed through architecture, music and drama.

Not only in worship does the mature pilgrim find consolation and inspiration, but in the fellowship which comes with those like-minded individuals who gather to celebrate life and to say their vows. The fellowship of the church is God high and man wide. It defies time and space. One lonely individual in the midst of a congregation becomes a part of all who have gone before him across the centuries, as well as a part of all those who will succeed him in future millennia. He is joined with the family of God in every nation on this little planet. He is no longer alone, but able to love and to be loved in that colony of heaven called the congregation. He hears again the call of Christ undiminished by rolling centuries.

Retired persons are particularly helpful in the educational ministry of the church. The rich experience of many years enables a citizen of the golden years to bring a vital message to the young, thereby bridging the gap between the generations and extending God's community of love on earth. Old people make great teachers. They also make great students. The vast library called *The Bible* is not easy to master. Retirement is a great time for a person to hear again the powerful message of the Hebrew Prophets, the stately music of the Psalms, the thrilling stories of the Patriarchs, the matchless biography of the Gospels, the intriguing history of the early church, the wide-ranging insights of the Epistles.

That person who does not know the meaning of the Ten Commandments of Moses or the beatitudes of Christ has deprived himself of God's everlasting revelation to man. To learn the history of the Judeo-Christian faith is itself a great joy. The cathedrals and temples of the world take on meaning when a person studies the symbolism and the history which they embody. Nobody is too old to share in this adventure and to give witness to those who have missed the splendor of God's presence.

One of the most remarkable aspects of any person's life is his religion. It is his deepest commitment to that which he believes. It is his cosmic loyalty which transcends all history and all human loyalties. It is both private and corporate. It is a message of redemption for our sins, of consolation for our sorrows and of hope for our destinies. "Faith," said Paul, "is the substance of things hoped for, the reality of things not seen." The person who lives by faith need not fear the everlasting shadow.

The renewed persons who exemplify the promise of the Prophet Isaiah, "But they that wait upon the Lord shall renew their strength; they shall mount up with wings as eagles ...," do not face death merely with resignation. On eagle wings of faith they go soaring over the valley of the shadow of death. Their influence goes on with family, friends, acquaintances and in history. Their identities are completed in that they are reunited with God, the creator, God, the redeemer, and God, the saviour.

CONCENTRATE THE MIND WONDERFULLY

T he celebrated literary guru, Samuel Johnson, made the remark —
"When a man knows he is to be hanged
in a fortnight, it concentrates
his mind wonderfully."[1]

One late October day I was headed for a bank investment seminar when I found myself hemorrhaging. My wife drove me to the hospital emergency room where I was admitted for surgery. The operation on the subsequent day disclosed a malignant tumor. Tests revealed that Cancer had invaded one of my ribs.

Dr. Johnson was right — this experience "concentrates the mind wonderfully!"

Now that I am living in that golden sunset afternoon of life. I have not yielded to despair. The turning seasons of color have never been more beautiful — daffodils on the hills in springtime, the quivering

---

1 Boswell, *Life of Johnson,* Sept. 19, 1777.

leafy shadows of a summer day, the autumn when echelons of wild geese pass by my window, and the first snowfall which comes down gently with deep symbolic implication. The joy and meaning of life that come from family and friends remind me that Goethe was right when he said, "To love and to be loved is the greatest thing in the world."

I do not intend to leave this beautiful life without a struggle. I can accept death with good grace when it is inevitable, but until then I shall live with zest, joy and service to those around me. I am very pleased to tell anyone that the diagnosis of an incurable disease is not the end; it is the beginning of a golden opportunity.

The days, the weeks, and now the years go by and I am able to "mount up with wings as eagles" in defiance of the dire predictions and early fears. Norman Cousins was right: A powerful will to live and a sensible cooperation between patient and physician can accomplish wonders![2]

I am fully aware of the recent findings of some researchers who have concluded that attitude has very little to do with my recovery from Cancer. My personal experience, and that of my close friends who have similar maladies, indicate otherwise. As one of my cherished friends, Janet Henry of Cleveland, said after she had lived twenty years beyond her predicted survival, "I have not only come to believe in miracles, but to *expect* them!" The sheer joy of being alive is more intense now than ever before. I have discovered that the greatest

---

2 Cousins, Norman: *Anatomy of an Illness as Perceived by the Patient, Reflections on Healing and Regeneration;* W.W. Norton & Company, Inc., New York (Bantam Books 1981).

renewal of life can come with some devastating and ominous discovery such as I and many of my contemporaries now face.

At fourscore years I have learned many things. I have discovered that life is a series of renewals. "Renewal" is a very big word. It means not only "to restore," but it implies a new beginning. It involves the surrender of those things that have served their time. It not only means regeneration in the physical sense, but it implies a renewed will to live.

Life is a struggle. As a brave pilgrim faces the issues and comes out victorious, there is a new wave of satisfaction, and even joy, as one moves on toward self-fulfillment. Every living organism must find this kind of renewal from time to time or perish.

In his essay, *"Vis Medicatrix Dei,"* Dr. Richard Cabot of Harvard Medical School found great comfort in postmortem examinations in which he discovered that many of the people who had lived a full lifetime had been at the edge of death with some unusually fatal disease, such as tuberculosis, impaired kidney function or Cancer — all without their knowledge. He mentions one 64-year-old man, killed by a truck, who would have been expected to die by at least four different maladies — tuberculosis in both lungs, cirrhosis of the liver, chronic kidney trouble and hardening of the arteries. Yet, the man had not known of any illness in his entire life.

Almighty God, working through nature and through the knowledge of science, together with the

---

3 Cabot, Richard, M.D. and Russell L. Dicks, B.D., *The Art of Ministering to the Sick,* Macmillan, New York, (1936) p. 118 ff.

arts and skills of the physicians, can bring on healing beyond our wildest imagination. I take great comfort in the fact that some of the cells in my body are fighting to protect me from the erratic growth of cells that will kill. As I go about my work of writing and lecturing, my immune system is battling to save my life.

God wants me to live, and I am cooperating to the best of my ability.

I have discovered that any person's life cycle moves forward in surges, rather than steady increments. Note, if you will, what happens to a young person who falls in love. The whole inner world of the young lover is more beautiful. A similar thing happens to the young adult who finds great satisfaction and success in a new career. There is a great leap forward for the person who is cured of a malady and finds the excitement and inner satisfaction of vibrant health. Any glorious new surprise can bring new joy to life.

For those of us who manage to overcome the challenges brought on by the different stages of life, and who move forward in the life cycle, the renewals keep on coming. The greatest renewal of all, I have found, came when I looked full into the face of death in my eightieth year.

The will to live is a primary drive for every organism. Schopenhauer once observed that the ear is an objectified desire to hear — the legs an objectified desire to run. To paraphrase that astute German philosopher who wrote *The World As Will And Idea* and who viewed reality in terms of will, one could say, "Aging is the objectified will to live."

We love to pretend that we are young, even when the wrinkles appear and the bones ache. We dissuade those who would admit to growing old. This is a social convention fraught with serious error. The greatest priority of any organism is survival, and being alive means growing older every day. The late Konrad Adenauer, famed leader of German political and economic recovery, approaching the age of ninety, was impatient with his personal physician who was unable to cure the Chancellor's heavy cold. The harrassed physician said, "I'm not a magician. I cannot make you young again!" I haven't asked you to," retorted the Chancellor, "All I want is to go on getting older!"

The will to live drives us on to stay alive as long as possible. Even when people say they wish to die, the old organs keep on working. My mother, ninety-three years old, deaf, blind and tired, clung to live as best she could while protesting that it was time for her to close out her long life.

When some of my colleagues in Gerontology speak of the later stages of the life cycle in terms of preparation for death, I find them in error. Longfellow was right when, in his "Psalm of Life", he said —

> *"Life is real, life is earnest,*
> *And the grave is not its goal."*

I most heartily agree with Montaigne, who argues that we need not study death in preparation for the end of life. Our goal is to live as long as possible, as well as possible and with as much fulfillment as possible.

Most of our conventional opinions about aging are dead wrong. We assume that aging starts at about mid-life and becomes a dominant concern at about retirement time. This is all wrong. Aging is lifelong. I was aging very rapidly at two or three years old when I fell into the settling pond of our California property! The thousands of students I have known in more than fifty years of teaching were all aging, every one. Any living organism is in the process of growing old. There are no exceptions.

RENEWAL IN CRISIS

Any kind of major crisis can become an opportunity for renewal. It need not be the discovery of an incurable disease. It can be any life event that brings with it an importunate demand for reappraisal, review and plan of action.

Many have faced crippling heart attacks with a resulting diminution of power and life expectancy. One of my most cherished friends was in a recent automobile accident which not only brought pain, discomfort and disability, but a severe reduction in life expectancy. A crippling stroke may be even more difficult to deal with since it can temporarily impair ability to make decisions.

Crises to confront us mortals are possibilities everywhere and always. Each of these events, devastating as they are, can be followed by an amazing and creative renewal. The loss of money, the loss of love, the shock of defeat and the loss of employment are among the blows that can bring opportunity. Serendipitous success, in like manner, can rearrange and improve the quality of life. It is possible for those spared from death or serious injury to awaken to new meaning and new achievements.

Out of my own long experience, I hope to show something of the range of quality of renewal that comes from my bout with Cancer. I have enjoyed one renewal after another throughout my lifetime, but this one is the best of all. My first response when the shock came was an overwhelming desire to go on living. I now have a message for those tempted to yield to despair. I confidently expect to live on for a few more years. I am feeling well and the Cancer is in recession. The hope, which I learned at my mother's breast, has never been as bright. Instead of depression and surrender, I have taken a new lease on life. My old bones that have weathered seven decades and more may have some cancerous cells in them, but they have rallied to a new fight for life, and I am confident that life will prevail.

This little poem describes something of my renewal in the face of disastrous news:

THE WAYWARD CELLS

If I can live a few more years
Sustained by hope and free from fears
Family and friends will keep me strong
And God will hear my thankful song

Life I have loved far more than most
This lovely world has been my host
I greet with joy each passing day
And hope that death will stay away

I view the past and count the cost
Of some things won and others lost
I know the pain of loss and strife
But have not lost my lust for life

Each rolling season will be new
When my terrestrial days are through
The Lord remembers every day
Though mortals let them slip away

I have no rendezvous with death
I cling to life with every breath
The Lord will find me when I'm gone
A dauntless eagle flying on!

Perry E. Gresham

My scholarly academic colleague, Erik Erikson, has, in my opinion, more than anyone else, shown the true nature of the later stages in the life cycle. He has taught the world the meaning of human growth and development utilizing the perceptive art film of Ingmar Bergman, called "Wild Strawberries." This is the study of a wise old physician who is honored for meritorious service by the University of Lund in Sweden. On the way to the honor convocation, the doctor has occasion to visit his old home and to reconstruct his childhood and youth. The wise old physician was no mean psychiatrist, and his self-analysis had depth. This brings him peace of mind, a better understanding of himself and a better attitude toward the world, his family and friends.[4]

Erikson calls this late stage of the life cycle the age of wisdom won through integrity. Every person who faces up to the fact of human mortality has opportunity to review the entire cycle of a lifetime in search of meaning, identity and self-fulfillment. Dr. Erikson's newest book, in collaboration with Joan Erikson and Helen Kivnick, reports on a series of case studies in which old people of the California Bay area have reached back into their past lives to recover a sense of meaning and integrity — these adventures into past experiences tend to bring wisdom.

I have reviewed my entire lifetime and have brought it all together with a resulting sense of meaning, integrity and wisdom. I fully understand my own mortality, but I have also found renewal of

---

4   Erikson, Erik H., *Adulthood*, W.W. Norton & Company, Inc., New York (1978), pp. 1-30.

the will to live and an exciting new beginning. I find joy in this very day, since it is the first day of the rest of my life.

The life pilgrimage of every person is a thrilling story. There is a novel in every lifetime, if it could be brought out with appropriate art and meaning. My own life has been filled with drama, with a full share of defeats and struggles, as well as some delightful surprises. My present struggle with Cancer involves many sleepless nights in which fears are magnified and dreams are strange and troublesome.

In my effort to keep a positive approach and to share this encouragement with my friends, I must guard to avoid understanding the inward battle against discouragement, despair and disgust. Many of my fears are ungrounded. Each time I feel a new pain, I wonder if it could be another tumor. My recovery is complicated by the recurrent smashes of pain from Tic Douloureux, which has been my scourge for twenty years; it has outlived three extensive surgeries from highly-qualified neurosurgeons.

Through it all, I have continued with hope and faith which came to me in my early years and which sustain me now. My message of renewal is not mere optimism nor shallow cheerfulness. I know the depth of discouragement and the intensity of pain. I have learned to flinch, but not to yield to despair. I shall keep on fighting the good fight.

What does a person do when faced with disease, loss, tragedy or defeat? The answer is that from this crisis can come the rewarding self-fulfillment of rediscovery as to who we are, what we are and what we long to be. Even more, we find out where we have been, for the life cycle has long dimensions. Popular songs are forever dealing with memories. The reason is clear. Some of life's richest satisfactions are derived from the early dreams, achievements and events in our lives. Recollections, reflections and reveries that come from memory expose the error of our common assumption that aging belongs only to the last stages of life. The beauty and meaning of growing old, as well as the quality of life which it encourages, comes from the entire life cycle which involves long memories of half-forgotten events of childhood, youth and middle years. No person is merely "old." The golden years are made up of lifelong echoes and overtones. My beautiful friend, Alice Truscon, "Nightingale of the Great Lakes," has sung "Memories" from the musical show "Cats" all over the land. As she sings the role of Grizabella The Glamor Cat her lovely voice intones —

"I remember the time
I knew what happiness was —
Let the memories live again"

My cherished and dedicated wife, who is my contemporary, is just now bringing together her autobiographical notes. These will mean everything to family and close friends, but most of all, this effort is her search for self-knowledge and integrity. She is reaching back into the half-forgotten previous stages of life.

Another aspect of crisis renewal is the sense of urgency. When we assume we shall just keep on living, we procrastinate. The friend is not called, the letter is not written and the financial transaction is delayed. Too many of our opportunities are *"manana*-ed away. When one realizes, however, that there may be but few years left, things get done, priorities are established and the resulting achievements bring immense satisfaction.

Estate planning is something that one hopes to do sometime, until the realization breaks in that the end may be near. At that time the planning occurs, The Will is written and financial arrangements are accomplished. Every life needs to be tidied up with regard to arrangements, such as disposal of property, appropriate answers to persistent questions and messages that need to be dispatched. When the days grow short one tends to speed accomplishment. A startling experience is a great motivator!

Everyone has long-unfulfilled interests and desires. I have felt keen interest in sharing my views about aging with my contemporaries. Now I am busy writing about some of these views because my time may not hold out. I have long wished to write a lively account of the life of Sir Thomas Gresham. I even have a subtitle for the book when and if — "An Elizabethan Success Story." This great merchant commoner was on intimate terms with four English monarchs. When he died he was accounted the richest man in England. He had protected the financial integrity of the Realm. Now that I have some discouraging health news, I shall get busy on the book.

My friend, whoever you are, whatever you wish to do, when some crisis forces you to consider your priorities move forward promptly and without delay. The great words of successful aging are — "DO IT NOW".

One of my late friends was a great golfer. He talked to me year after year about his desire to play the famous Saint Andrews Course in Scotland.

Resolve was modest and delay seemed always justified by more urgent matters. When he discovered, however, that his life might be much shorter than he had assumed, he embarked on the Canadian Pacific steamer for Scotland. He found the "auld course" to be very ordinary, but for him, very exciting. I doubt that I have found a happier friend than was my golfing companion who had realized a lifelong desire. He lived only a few more years, but he heard "the late lark singing."

When George Romney, famed English painter, realized the danger of his recurrent fever, he returned to Mary Abbott, the landlady's daughter whom he had married in his youth but abandoned when he became famous. He forgot about his honors in London and Paris and returned to his rustic wife. Mary Abbott was saint enough to take him back. She had patiently waited for him all these years. His life ended in her loving care. His brilliant career had become history, and he died without a sense of despair and loss. The shock he experienced with a life-threatening disease saved him.

A sobering crisis not only concentrates the mind; it can bring on a new and vital religious devotion. Everyone has some sort of religion. Its nature and practice are related to childhood experiences. Religion deals with ultimate loyalties which are above and beyond the public order of life. Faith and hope go beyond the life cycle. No mortal can find complete fulfillment in one short lifetime. The most ultimate concerns are reserved for the Realm above and beyond history.

Let no one make light of foxhole religion, death-bed religion, or any kind of religious commitment that comes in the face of the ending life cycle.

Religion can be vital and relevant in times of strength and youth, but perhaps even more sustaining in the face of death. The religious ideals, fears, hopes and beliefs develop in childhood and continue throughout a human existence. When crisis comes these half-forgotten feelings, impulses, beliefs and values come flooding back. The discipline of sophisticated living may add new dimensions. The renewal of religious faith in the face of crisis is richer and wiser than at any other time in life. When Rudyard Kipling was facing death, his sophisticated life experience gave additional meaning to his childhood faith. When one of his colleagues asked at the end of his life what he really wanted, he answered, "I want my Heavenly Father."

After fifty years of teaching philosophy, I can say, with all candor, that I face the end of life with more faith and hope and trust than at any other time in my busy career. The majesty of the Psalm, "Lord, thou hast been our dwelling place in all generations," is for me like comforting and compelling rumbles of thunder on the western hills. Regardless of any religious background, each of us can find a rich and rewarding renewal of faith when the lightning stroke of crisis is at hand.

Most of us long for some kind of immortality. To live in the memory of God above and beyond history is not enough to fulfill the wishes and aspirations of anyone who would like to be remembered on Earth. The Pyramids of Egypt, the Tombs of Italy and the Presidential Libraries in America reach out for a long memory and, if possible, a place in history. We hope we will be remembered for a considerable period of time after the life cycle is concluded. Family and friends, and noble deeds live on, of course. Life is worthy of long remembrance. God remembers, even if friends and relatives forget. No Taj Mahal, no Pyramid and no Presidential Library is necessary. Every good life is an abiding memorial.

Everyone would do well to write a letter or two worthy of long remembrance. Placed in the appropriate hands, these letters can perhaps be handed down from generation to generation. Those who paint, write or compose should leave a legacy of art. The endless resourcefulness of the inventive human spirit can devise the means for those who truly long to be remembered. My contemporary, Dr. Harold Lyman of Salem, Oregon, who retired as a parish minister a decade or so ago, will be remembered for the beautiful clocks he has fashioned from the great trees of the Pacific Northwest. There is a touch of immortality about the time which his clocks report.

Crisis renewal is for anybody. For the person who anticipates death, but lives on for many years, the sunset is more beautiful and exciting. For those of us who may come to a quicker end, the renewal is the last, and best, consolation. One absolute *sine qua non* for such a renewal is a means by which a person can escape from the distasteful accumulation of regrets, guilt feelings, self-blame and humiliations. Every human being is subject to sins, mistakes, stupidities, injuries, insensitivities and feelings of aggression, even if the deeds are repressed. How then does one deal with this problem? From an old German ritual comes a partial answer.

Out in the ranch country of Colorado, where I did some creative aging in my early teens, we had a community bonfire around the first of May each year. My Pennsylvania Dutch grandmother told me that the custom came down from Walpurgisnight, still celebrated in the German mountains as "The Witches Sabbath." This fire figures prominently in Goethe's story of "Faustus." In The Divide Country of my boyhood, the community fire served as a kind of exorcising ritual to rid the participants of distasteful trash or reminders of failure, guilt, gloom or folly. This is not a wooded country and we could spare no trees, so trash was saved up in anticipation of the great bonfire. My grandmother told me of one family whose children they feared had been contaminated by body lice. The infested clothing was carefully isolated in a bundle and pitched into the campfire for utter destruction. One lush old rancher brought a jug of whiskey, half-full, to pitch into the great white heat and be remembered no more. He may have repeated the ritual on the subsequent year. One harried ranch wife, whose good-for-nothing husband had left her, declared her independence by throwing her tear-stained marriage certificate into the fire. All sorts of mementos that were bitter to remember were hoarded with the highly flammable trash for the Walpurgisnight fire which would light up the western sky.

This sort of symbolic ritual would be a great thing for any person who faces the facts of mortality. To take every grudge, each hate, all feelings of guilt, every self-condemnation for foolish behavior having been shrived by faith and disciplined by appropriate penance, followed by the glorious and cleansing feeling of forgiveness, should be cast into the symbolic bonfire completely consumed and remembered no more.

A far better means of purification from feelings of guilt, regret for mistakes, painful memories of humiliation and failure, and other burdens, is the

Church, the Synagogue or the Temple. For rolling centuries altars have invited the weary pilgrims to confess their sins to Almighty God, to find forgiveness and to leave the negative psychological impedimenta at the altar. Penitence, confession and a humble petition invites forgiveness. The religions of mankind throughout world history have been specialists in proclaiming forgiveness, which covers regret with the Divine mantle of charity.

Perhaps this is what Alfred North Whitehead had in mind when he said, "Religion is force of belief cleansing the inward parts."

Perry E. Gresham
President Emeritus and
Distinguished Professor
Bethany College
Bethany, West Virginia